The BRAVE LEADER

More courage. Less fear.
Better decisions for
inclusive leadership.

DAVID McQUEEN

First published in Great Britain by Practical Inspiration Publishing, 2024

ISBN   9781788604536   (paperback)
            9781788605779   (hardback)
            9781788604550   (epub)
            9781788604543   (mobi)

Want to bulk-buy copies of this book for your team and colleagues? We can customize the content and co-brand *The BRAVE Leader* to suit your business's needs.

Please email info@practicalinspiration.com for more details.

Practical Inspiration
Publishing

I would like to dedicate this book to my three musketeers – my wife Madeline and my daughters Rianna and Lauren.

Contents

Chapter 1

What Is Brave Leadership?

Hey you, my name is David McQueen. I am a leadership coach working with organizations in the non-profit and private sectors. Over the years, I have always coached my clients to be brave and courageous, to make difficult decisions, to think strategically and to create team or organizational cultures where that bravery can be replicated.

I have written snippets about my approach on my blog, posted short-form articles on LinkedIn, and I have given insights on my podcast and as a guest on other podcasts.

For many years, people have asked me to write a book explaining my approach and why inclusive leadership is so important to me and the people I work with. And so here we are.

I would like to start off with my definitions of 'leadership' and the lesser-known term 'followership'.

Before I do, I should clearly state that I don't believe leadership is restricted to the workplace. I have personally seen it show up in martial arts classes, football matches, youth groups, community projects and faith groups. Limiting it to the workplace is somewhat myopic, but I do understand why many people only think of it in that context. And so even though the focus of this book is on leadership in the workplace, or organizational leadership as it is often referred to, leadership can apply just as well outside the workplace.

The truth is there is much more written about management than there is about leadership. As a practitioner in this space who has read a huge amount on the subject, way too much of the literature just focuses on feel-good messages, presenting ideas and ideals that don't really work in the real world. Or if they do, there is little to no data to back this up.

There are scholars who have questioned the direction that the leadership development industry is going in. The scholar Barbara Kellerman did this in *The End of Leadership* and Dr Jeffrey Pfeffer did the same in *Leadership BS.* The aim of this book is less about questioning the leadership industry and more about getting you to explore and reflect on your own impact as a leader – or if you are an aspiring leader, what you would like your impact to be – and to look at the expectations you have about those who lead you.

So let's jump in with some definitions.

Defining leadership

Here are some different definitions of leadership:

- 'the action of leading a group of people or an organisation' *(Oxford English Dictionary)*;
- 'the accomplishment of a goal through the direction of human assistants' (W.C.H. Prentice);[1] and
- 'the capacity of a human community to shape its future' (Peter Senge et al).[2]

My favourite of these is the definition by Peter Senge. While I see value in the other definitions, this is the one closest to my way of thinking. It goes beyond thinking of leadership as some single act by a person or persons to focus more on how

---

[1] See a reprint of Prentice's 1961 article: W.C.H. Prentice 'Understanding leadership', *Harvard Business Review.* Available from: https://hbr.org/2004/01/understanding-leadership [accessed 24 September 2023].

[2] P. Senge, A. Kleiner, C. Roberts, G. Ross and B. Smith, *The Dance of Change: The Challenges to Sustaining Momentum in Learning Organizations* (1999).

a community shapes what happens next. This can relate to a formal or informal group of people working together.

When I am approached by people to be their leadership coach, I am curious as to what they actually mean when they use the word 'leadership'. I ask them the following questions: What do they think I can bring to the table? Are they confusing being an executive with being a leader? Why do they think that managers or bosses are different from leaders? Do they see leadership as a function or a title? Do they think they are leaders?

In this book, I want to explore the concept of leadership through the eyes of the individual, through teams and through the organization. I want to look at what it really is and what impact it makes, and the specific things that make leadership effective and sustainable.

For me, leadership focuses on guiding, influencing and inspiring others towards the achievement of common goals. It involves making sense of the world around you, making decisions, providing direction and motivating individuals or teams to work together towards a shared vision.

One of my favourite framings of leadership comes from Kellerman's *The End of Leadership* where she speaks about the 'equilateral triangle' for leadership – you need context, leaders and followers as equal sides of that triangle. This approach really resonates with the way I see things.

Context matters when it comes to leadership, and we need to understand the unique settings where leadership is played out. What works in an army won't translate directly into a manufacturing company. What works in a hospital won't translate into the airline industry.

In any organization, there is a set of norms, values and circumstances that shape the way things are done. From the corporate institution that focuses on how to make money for its shareholders to the non-profit organization that is thinking about how to make an impact for its stakeholders, or the civic society that is concentrating on serving the community – all these have their own organizational influences.

Outside the organization, there are other influences – such as technology, laws, compliance standards, societal trends and norms – that will shape the context for leadership within the organization. Think of the laws that have shaped rights for working parents or the political movements that have shaped the way people think.

So context, both internal and external to the organization, shapes the way leaders behave in an organization. For example, leaders in fast-growth companies will need to make robust decisions rapidly. They may have to make unpopular decisions in order to get the job done. This can lead to tension if people don't understand the pressures of this context. On the other hand, in organizations where the emphasis is less on growth, leaders may be able to think more about collaboration and take time to deliberate on different courses of action.

The third part of Kellerman's triangle, followers, is less spoken about than leadership, so I will define that next.

Defining followership

Followership involves those who are actively participating in the vision, mission and goals set by leaders. So while leadership focuses on guiding and influencing others, followership emphasizes the role of individuals who willingly follow and support those leaders.

Effective followership isn't passive. It requires participation and alignment with those who lead. In an ideal world, followers would be able to offer up ideas, insights and expertise to enhance their organizations' overall performance and outcomes.

Ideally, followers demonstrate trust and loyalty towards their leaders and their organizations. They believe in the leaders' vision and values, and they remain committed and dedicated to achieving shared goals. Critically, they expect the same trust and loyalty from those who lead them.

Followership requires collaboration. Even in the most hierarchical organizations, followers need to be adaptable and flexible in responding to changing circumstances. They must be willing to adjust their approaches, roles and responsibilities to support the overall success of the organization.

Followers provide constructive feedback and offer suggestions for improvement when necessary. This works when the leaders in the organization provide space for it to happen because they understand the symbiosis between themselves and their followers.

I often ask people, during my talks and when I'm coaching, what they understand followership to be. Very often I am met with this weird look, like what the heck is this dude on about? Like I just made the word up.

It's interesting though, isn't it? Given that so many people wax lyrical about leadership and have unrealistic expectations in relation to the 'great leader', very little is said about followership or the impact of a 'great follower'.

Where would historical narratives of figures like Joan of Arc, Jesus of Nazareth, Napoleon Bonaparte, Adolf Hitler, Benito Mussolini, Toussaint Louverture or Mary Seacole be had there not been a group of followers enabling or supporting their leadership. Be it political, corporate, non-profit, educational or spiritual, there is a fundamental need to understand the importance of followership.

It is even more important to understand that even for you as a leader, there is still someone guiding you. This might be someone you follow directly – perhaps the chair of your organization, a senior person in government, an influential investor or stakeholder – or someone you follow indirectly – a role model or a fire warden.

The point to take away here is that it is important to understand the people you are leading so that you can tailor your leadership style accordingly.

Inclusive leadership

Have you ever heard the term 'inclusive leadership'? Does it mean anything to you?

I define inclusive leadership as the ability of leaders, at all levels, to:

- attract, empower and support talent to achieve a vision or goal, and do so without marginalizing any of them; and
- define, develop and maintain systems and processes that are sensitive to the needs of stakeholders – this applies to functional areas of an organization, including product, customer service, sales and talent.

I include that second part of the definition because organizations often only focus on talent management, whereas I believe that they should aim for inclusive leadership across the organization, to reduce marginalization in all areas.

Of course, even if this is understood, organizations won't always get it right.

My definition takes a broader view than most definitions of leadership by also considering customers. Any business or organization should prioritize its customers' needs, right? So leadership should intend not to exclude or marginalize them.

Very often when exploring definitions of leadership, like those mentioned earlier, there is not much of an effort to look at it through the lens of inclusion. I believe that more leaders need to do this.

For me, inclusive leadership is the best way to ensure support right across the organization. It gets us to look for the best means of serving our customers. It goes to the heart of product development, marketing, hiring and retention, innovation, financial management and all the essential areas of business that make organizations successful. And at the heart of this is a system of thinking and decision-making that allows organizations to be successful and sustainable.

Too often, inclusive leadership can be interpreted narrowly in the sense of attracting, retaining and promoting talent from all backgrounds. This is a good thing, but for me this is just the start of the conversation around what true inclusive leadership looks like. We need to broaden our remit somewhat to make sure that it's not just about talent management but also embraces other parts of the organization. (I talk about this in detail later on in the book.)

Fundamentally, to be an inclusive leader requires *bravery*.

It requires you to have bags of courage to challenge some of the more traditional approaches to leadership.

The kind of courage that allows you to state your case when someone tells you to cut corners when developing a product.

The kind of courage that makes you question whether you are making a choice based on the best data available.

The kind of courage that makes you hold your ground when you know that a decision-making process is not sustainable and could have a detrimental impact if pursued for short-term gain.

The kind of courage that allows you to share your insights on talent management even if colleagues or other stakeholders describe your approach as 'woke'.

The kind of courage that allows you to stick to your principles even if fraudulent or unethical financial practices have kept the organization afloat.

Defining BRAVE leadership

In 2020, I ended up working with only about 10% of the people who had made enquiries for my talks and coaching. When they approached me, I would ask them a few challenging questions to see how serious they were: Why did you call me to speak to your staff? What plans do you have in place to actively measure impact when I am gone? Are you booking me because you are scared of appearing racist? (For context, this was around the time George Floyd died in the United States, and some people wanted help to address organizational issues related to race.) Have you had conversations with your staff about how you are going to ride through this pandemic? How willing are you to make change?

When I asked these sorts of questions, I would see the blood drain from people's faces or their eyes open wide. I would see potential clients wanting to say 'what the heck kind of question is that?'

I believe it is important to work with people who are willing to consider these difficult questions, people who can say that, even though they don't have the answers yet, they will make the effort to think things through. Even if it is scary, they will be courageous enough to explore the possibilities.

I decided to explain to them what 'BRAVE leadership' was about and why it was important.

In doing this, I started with dictionary definitions of 'brave' and found that it can be used as:

- an adjective – showing mental or moral strength to face danger, fear or difficulty;
- a verb – to face or endure with courage; and
- a noun – a person with a mental or moral strength to face danger, fear or difficulty.

Synonyms for the word 'brave' include intrepid, fearless, undaunted and gutsy. This is how I wanted leaders to think of not only themselves but also their teams, their followers and the organizations that they were part of. This helped to shape the model that I have used when working with clients, and frame it as an acronym: BRAVE.

The BRAVE acronym

The BRAVE acronym stands for Bold, Resilient, Agile, Visionary and Ethical. These five pillars provide the grounding for the kinds of sense-making, decision-making, strategic thinking and actions that drive inclusive leadership. It is not a linear five-part thing that all clients have to tick off on a list, but rather a simple model, a set of prompts to focus the mind.

Bold

To be Bold is to willingly make decisions, to take risks and to act innovatively with confidence and courage.

Being Bold, especially when your opinion is not the most popular, is not straightforward at all. Being Bold enough to change your own behaviour is hard. You may feel cognitive load, wondering whether being Bold will be seen as being aggressive, when the intention is to be assertive. Feedback might suggest that your being Bold makes people uncomfortable. A lot of it is contextual as well. For leaders from under-represented backgrounds, being Bold can be especially hard where they do not receive the same treatment as other leaders.

One of my clients had a horrible habit of interrupting women in senior management meetings, despite claiming to give agency to female colleagues. I observed this in both Zoom and in-person meetings. He never did it when men were speaking. I mentioned this to him and initially he was quite defensive about it, saying things like 'I'm not here to be politically correct but to get the job done.' I was fully aware that it was not his intention to offend. But rather than be distracted by his defensiveness, I asked him what he would do if he was confronted by someone he had spoken over. Would he be courageous enough to admit that he was doing this and that it was potentially disempowering those who he *claimed* to give agency to?

It was painful to watch him squirm in his seat when he was challenged. Other members of his team would remind him of his mantra that all voices were valid, and that he should listen to what was being said so that others might respond rather than react. However, some of his peers told me that there was no chance he would back down, because he wasn't courageous enough to admit when he was wrong. Still, I persisted and bit by bit he started to make small changes. He is still a work in progress and recognizes that a part of inclusive leadership is making tough and Bold changes.

As I explain later in the book, a lot of leadership hangs on the norms and expectations that exist in the organization. If the organization doesn't value Boldness, the leader who seeks to be Bold will face extra challenges.

Resilient

Resilience is the human capacity to meet adversity, setbacks and trauma, and then recover from them in order to be present and productive. It is about managing your energy in order to keep going and inspire others.

Resilient leadership is a team sport. It cannot fall on the shoulders of one person. That is a recipe for ruin, because what would happen if that person were to leave the team or the organization? As well as building an appetite for risk and change in your team or organization, it is important to think about the practices that are necessary to maintain this. Given how rapidly things change in our hyper-connected world, this is an essential part of being able to thrive.

This part of the model gets leaders to really explore what strengths lie within their team, or others they influence, and how these can be rallied to strengthen the team as a whole. The reason we focus here on the team is that we are looking for the collective response to situations. Those individuals who can demonstrate Resilience will in turn impact the ability of others to pull through in tough times.

There have been times when I have witnessed teams being blindsided by political or economic events that are totally outside their control. A client who worked in insurance, fearing that the decisions they took would end up alienating groups they had pledged to work with, decided to take a moment and ask themselves and their team: 'What decisions will we be proud of when we look at them three to four years down the line?' This was in the face of the communications and PR departments wanting to act on the issues in the moment. This client believed it was important that the team could take unpopular decisions, and team members were reminded that the values and beliefs that took them through difficult situations before would steer them through choppy times again.

It can be way too easy to get distracted in the moment and forget to foster the kind of team or organizational culture which brings strength. This pillar serves as a reminder that in your work as leaders (and as followers), being able to bounce back from more challenging situations is important.

Agile

I define agility as the ability of leadership to adapt to changing circumstances both inside and outside their organizations.

In my work in leadership development over the last ten years, I have come across many situations where organizational leaders have had to review the more traditional approaches to strategy, long-term planning and organizational change. Many of these approaches were appropriate for a different time. Yet being able to sit down with a team and plan a five-year strategy in anticipation of changes in the world outside the organization is often deemed a luxury, an exercise in vanity, as things change so much.

As I write this, I think of the way events like the COVID-19 pandemic, the Russian invasion of Ukraine, the Black Lives Matter protests, the climate change crisis and a host of other social, political and economic events have forced organizations to think quickly on their feet. This does not mean that strategy, long-term planning and organizational change are redundant – it is still very important to have these things in place in order to grow sustainable businesses. What is at challenge here is the ability of the organization to react to external challenges.

One of my clients had seen a few years of growth in his tech firm. As for many companies in this field, the pandemic had provided a spike in the new business. In order to meet this surge in demand, he and his team had made strides to increase the workforce across the organization.

Like so many other businesses, the ambitions of growth in his organization had been buoyed by the increased demand and by government attempts to stave off any worries by shoring up the economy. But as with all economic cycles, what goes up must come down, and there came a point when the bloat of overhead costs, mainly in salaries, was not sustainable as the company couldn't generate income at the same pace it used to. These new headwinds meant that this organization had to make a significant part of the workforce redundant.

Whether we call it downsizing, restructuring, salary realignment or any of the other fancy terms used for mass sackings and redundancies, laying off staff is never easy. Well, for most people anyway. Agility as pillar of the BRAVE model is a combination of being courageous enough to make tough decisions while also thinking about how those decisions are implemented and the impact this has on people.

Running any organization – whether in the public, private or third sector – is no easy feat. For some organizations, being able to make good decisions and take quick and effective action is a must in order to stay efficient and competitive. The focus on agility here is to respond effectively and inclusively when faced with such challenges.

Visionary

To influence others, build trust, give those under leadership a sense of ownership in the plans of the organization, we should never underestimate the impact of a strong vision.

Visionary leadership focuses on what is to come, the trajectory that will shape the behaviour, culture and intent of the organization for some time.

Organizations are leaning into new ways of working. Lots of changes are happening socially, politically, economically and technologically. Leaders and organizations have to take into consideration things such as climate change, conflicts, environmental social and governmental policies, cross-cultural communication, inflation, disease and so many other factors that will impact how the organization not only survives but thrives in this ever-changing world.

There are clients I've worked with who have been reluctant to speak about being Visionary. They don't want to look too far ahead into the future. They want to be able to deal with just the here and now. The challenge I always give them is that if they don't have a vision for the future, how will they be able to handle when things do change, for better or for worse. And so, when we're talking about inclusive leadership, and especially being Visionary, there is a need for leaders across the board to have a vision about where the organization can go if all the resources, intelligence and innovation are leveraged to the max.

To use a quote from the Bible, 'where there is no vision, the people perish'.[3] This may sound harsh, but I think it's a good metaphor to help leaders understand how important it is to have a vision, or a direction, when leading.

Ethical

The fifth and final pillar of BRAVE is Ethical leadership.

From the jump, I think it is important to make a distinction between ethics and morals. Ethics, for the purpose of this book, are external rules. A way of seeing things driven by a collective. This might involve codes of conduct in workplaces or principles in religions. Morals refer to an individual's own principles regarding what's right and wrong. I mention this because it can be very easy to follow the ethical principles of an organization even when they are not in tune with your

---

[3] This is found in Proverbs 29:18.

own morals. Note also that being moral doesn't necessarily mean you are ethical.

I raise this distinction to explain why there can be a pushback against the way things are done in an organization and why a leader may experience resistance regardless of how they approach things.

Organizations have had to deal with lawsuits and implement internal disciplinary measures because of dissonance between what the organization sets out as being ethically right and what individuals see as being morally right.

One of the first principles or questions we explore as part of this model is sustainability in leadership. We dive into the detail of sustainable leadership in Chapter 6, but for the minute I will look at what things are sustainable within the context of Ethical leadership.

Let's say, for example, a company decides that as part of the supply chain they want to only work with organizations that source from a specific place, do no harm or at least try to reduce harm to the environment. Suppliers will be asked whether these principles have been adhered too. The Ethical pillar provides a lens for leaders to examine the decisions that are made.

What does ethics mean to the team and the organization? What specific Ethical behaviours are required of leaders? How do we determine how to make Ethical decisions? What are the consequences of unethical behaviour?

I strongly believe that organizational ethics can't be taught but they can be modelled. When I talk about Ethical leadership, I am referring to those codes of conduct that are helpful to other employees, customers or stakeholders impacted by your leadership. Just as doctors, lawyers or accountants have ethical codes, so too do organizations.

∼

Hopefully it makes sense to you why these five pillars form the model I use for coaching and facilitating with senior executive and management teams. It doesn't mean that I go through each one step by step when working with clients; rather, they offer a guide to allow my clients to think about how inclusive leadership works for them and those they lead.

The truth is anyone can create a model and trademark it (as I have done), but the science or thinking behind these models is what's important. So, in this book, I share the key coaching approaches that I lean on in order to deliver this model.

By now you should be able to see what BRAVE leadership is, the principles on which this form of inclusive leadership stands. And you should see that it moves beyond just thinking in terms of protected characteristics of talent to a more courageous way of thinking of how leadership presents itself across your organization.

This is what I explore in the next chapter.

Chapter 2

Leadership as a system

In each chapter of this book, my desire is to get you think like a BRAVE leader. Whether you're reading this as a team within your organization or as a group of leaders from different organizations, I want you to think about how you can make better decisions and how you can collaborate as much as possible to get the best results – for yourself as well as for your team or organization.

To think like a BRAVE leader, you need to see leadership as a *system* – what I call 'systemic leadership' – as opposed to individual acts (which might be acts of brilliance or balderdash!) by a single leader.

To create a system of consistent and sustainable leadership requires two things: the parking of overinflated ego in order to do a real, deep audit into how best to serve customers and stakeholders; and developing something that is replicable so that it can be implemented by others.

Now, having worked across the world with organizations in different sectors and disciplines, I can tell you first hand that getting people to buy into systemic leadership can be a very big challenge.

In principle, it might seem very straightforward to join the dots between different parts of an organization so that aims and processes are interconnected, but the reality is a bit tougher.

What is systemic leadership?

Systemic leadership goes beyond traditional leadership approaches by emphasizing a holistic understanding of organizations that takes account of the fact that organizational systems are dynamic. As a discipline and practice, this looks at how far leadership is interconnected, both internally and externally. It leans heavily on ideas around systems thinking – how systems can be used to navigate complexity and uncertainty and how systems enable organizations to achieve sustainable growth and success.

A big part of systemic leadership is being Ethical. This involves considering the broader impact of one's actions, making responsible decisions and promoting positive cultural practices within the organization.

Some of the more challenging problems that arise in my work, and the work of other coaches I talk to, centre around leaders operating in silos and not being interconnected. The challenges of not being able to identify patterns, analyse feedback loops and understand the consequences of actions for the entire system will always exist if you don't systemize your leadership.

Now, this is a lot easier said than done. It requires a lot of interaction between stakeholders to be able to make this work.

∼

I have drawn on a few authors to inform my own understanding and appreciation of systemic leadership and its impact. Three specific works stand out for me: *Leadership and the New Science* by Margaret J. Wheatley; *The Dance of Change* by Peter Senge et al; and *Leading from the Emerging Future* by Otto Scharmer and Katrin Kaufer.[4]

---

[4] M.J. Wheatley, *Leadership and the New Science: Discovering Order in a Chaotic World* (1994); P. Senge, A. Kleiner, C. Roberts, G. Ross and B. Smith, *The Dance of Change: The Challenges to Sustaining Momentum in Learning Organizations* (1999); and O. Scharmer and K. Kaufer, *Leading from the Emerging Future: From Ego-System to Eco-System Economies* (2013).

All of these books are very informative, but the last one, *Leading from the Emerging Future*, really impacted my thinking with some of its core concepts around systemic leadership. I welcome your patience as I explain why.

The first concept that stood out to me is 'Theory U', a framework for deep personal and collective transformation. This outlines a process called 'presencing', which involves blending sensing and mindfulness to tap into our highest future potential. Presencing helps leaders connect with their deeper sources of intelligence and wisdom.

The second concept is shifting from 'ego-system' to 'eco-system'. This refers to the need for a shift in leadership mindset away from ego-system thinking, which is self-centred and focused on individual goals and interests, and towards eco-system thinking, which considers the wellbeing of the whole system. Transformative leaders embrace eco-system thinking, considering the perspectives and needs of all stakeholders.

The third is deep listening and dialogue. Deep listening involves suspending one's assumptions, judgements and preconceived notions to genuinely hear and understand others. Dialogue creates spaces for diverse perspectives to emerge, facilitating collective intelligence and creative problem-solving.

The fourth one really aligns with the BRAVE pillar of being Visionary in that it encourages leaders to embrace a future-oriented mindset. Leaders seek to sense and connect to emerging possibilities rather than solely reacting to past patterns. Leaders cultivate the ability to sense the emerging future and shape it through their actions, thereby co-creating new realities.

Scharmer and Kaufer also introduce the concept of 'four levels of listening', which correspond to different qualities of attention. The levels are:

- *downloading* – listening to confirm existing beliefs;
- *factual listening* – listening for information;

- *empathic listening* – listening with empathy and openness; and
- *generative listening* – listening to uncover the emerging future, with an open mind and heart.

The book explores how to lead change in complex systems. It explores how transformative leaders navigate complexity and initiate systemic change. It presents tools and frameworks to help leaders identify key leverage points for transformative change within complex systems.

The book also considers the role of prototyping and learning in systemic leadership. It encourages leaders to engage in rapid prototyping and experimentation to test new ideas and approaches, to embrace a culture of learning and iterate based on feedback and insights gained from the prototyping process. This approach encourages adaptive and emergent solutions to complex problems.

Systemic leadership is not an easy path to take, but we can learn from academic works and from the frontline of organizations how to develop practical tools and strategies to design such systems.

The big question, I guess, is how do we apply these concepts and make sure that systemic leadership is BRAVE and inclusive.

One of my clients was really proud of having an 'open door' policy for colleagues. As a senior executive, he thought it was important that more junior staff were able to get access to him. He would gently mentor those who popped in to talk about careers or run an idea past him before speaking to their line managers.

That last part of the equation was a problem. Some reading this may be wondering how this could be problematic. Surely an open door policy is what organizations really want, right?

The problem arose when staff got way too comfortable approaching my client to 'soundboard' ideas, from performance and salary issues to process suggestions and product development ideas. It was only after I performed 360-degree feedback with some of the line managers of those staff members that my client realized there was a problem. Just in case you don't know what 360-degree feedback is, it is a system of feedback where you interview peers, managers and those who report to you, and sometimes even external stakeholders, about your ways of working.

There were several instances where the line managers (who were my client's direct reports) felt powerless to lead or manage their teams because those individuals had a get-out clause to go and speak to a senior leader (my client). This was despite my client having told the line managers they had final say in the sorts of issues that were coming up.

If something came up, it wasn't uncommon for a team member to tell their line manager that they had already run it past my client and he was OK with it; or they would be able to use tips he provided to negotiate with the line manager.

So while, on the face of it, this approach seems like a really great way of being able to mentor staff in the organization, on digging deeper into what was happening as a result, my client realized how he was starting to undermine the line managers. He realized how people would pull out the 'executive' card if there was a point of conflict and how, because he was in a position of power, it made the line manager's job much harder to convince their direct reports that the final decisions around pay, performance, holidays and processes lay with them.

So, based on the coaching work I have done, I can see that while there is nothing wrong with senior executives aiming to be somewhat accessible, it is important to consider how that affects leadership practices across the organization.

Systemic leadership recognizes that culture emerges from the collective behaviours, beliefs and values of individuals within the organization. By understanding the systemic nature of culture, leaders can influence its development and alignment with the organization's goals. When you model desired behaviours, communicate the organization's vision effectively and establish systems and structures that support the desired culture, you end up fostering a positive and inclusive culture – one which enhances employee satisfaction, productivity and overall organizational performance.

This focus on leadership being systemic, or having a recognizable DNA throughout the organization, is what I want to emphasize in this chapter. By promoting a culture of BRAVE leadership throughout an organization, BRAVE leaders can be encouraged and thrive.

The myth of the hero leader

There is a lot of hero worship when it comes to leadership, whether it be the hero commander, the hero CEO, the hero sports manager or the hero youth worker.

There are tips on how individuals can shine and do well by following the example of these hero leaders – doing the things which won *them* awards or had *them* featured on magazine covers or on social media listicles.

But who does this hero leader serve? Who dares to speak against or challenge this hero leader? Who holds the hero leader accountable when they are considered omnipotent, omniscient and without blame?

Far too often people have this view that leadership is just down to one heroic person, but it's not. Being able to see a more contextual and more nuanced view of leadership is important, and this is what inspired me to write more around BRAVE leadership. We don't need another lone hero. Rather, we need to create an environment where leadership is shared among a number of leaders so that we aren't dependent on just one person.

Barbara Kellerman, who I mentioned in Chapter 1, talks about three elements that demonstrate the *impact* of leadership – influence, power and authority.

These are not limited to individuals who have 'leader' in their job title, but can apply to anyone who gets to lead a group of people. Let's take the role of fire warden – the person (or persons) within an organization who has been designated the task of getting people out of a building should there be a fire.

If there is a fire drill or indeed a real fire in a building, at that moment the warden is the person best qualified to make sure that people follow instructions to exit the building as safely as possible. They have the uniform, the equipment – such as loudhailers – and the authority to make sure that things get done.

Regardless of your stature or role in a company, a fire warden can call to an end your senior executive meeting, sales call or product development exercise – any work process – if it is necessary to get you out of the building and safe. They have influence – we respect the fire warden. They have power – they can make the difference between being safe or not. And they have authority – by virtue of being assigned the role of fire warden.

I give this example because a fire warden doesn't have to fit the ideal of 'great leader'. They don't have to be charismatic. Heck, they don't even have to be a nice person. The role only requires that the individual is informed on the latest protocols around fire safety and that, when called to do so, they can lead all the people who depend on their wisdom and training to safety.

The fire warden is an example of leadership within a system.

We can think of the system here as workplace safety and compliance. This leadership role helps the organization fulfil its duty of care to staff. The people who don't comply with the leader will get their ass kicked or even suffer an injury. Ok that's an extreme example, but you get my point. The point is that in this sort of situation, regardless of a leader's personality or personal brand, their authority is not questioned, because they are working for the greater good of the people in the company.

Many of us who work in organizational leadership coaching can recall several tales of individual leaders who think they have to be a hero. Individuals who have read the literature or watched content around personal or leadership branding and feel that it is important they are seen as indispensable – as the person who is holding it all together for the success of their unit, division, country or organization! It takes a lot as a coach to stay centred and not roll your eyes when you hear these narratives.

My take has always been that it should be easy for those who follow you to be able to challenge you. Fairly, bravely and without fear of retribution.

Even more so, they should trust you because they believe in your ability to get the best out of them. They certainly shouldn't feel coercion to do what you say.

This throws a spanner in the works for some leaders. They will look you straight in the eye and say that none of their staff are afraid of them. And when presented with evidence that this is actually the case, one of the immediate reactions will be: 'Who said that?' They will try to figure out who raised the point so they can have a word.

We are all flawed as humans who can have inflated egos, and if we think that it's necessary to survive in the workplace, we may try to persuade others that we are indispensable. Systemic leadership, on the other hand, creates a container for the kind of leadership behaviours and standards expected from anyone who is asked to be in a position of leadership at any level across the company. Let's dive into that a bit more.

Developing an inclusive leadership system

Developing an inclusive leadership system is not a one-time event, but an ongoing process that requires commitment and effort from all levels of the organization. It requires understanding and a heck of a lot of energy to drive it forward. It requires all those in positions of leadership to understand their roles and the behaviours expected in those roles.

To map the effectiveness of a system requires courageous analysis of how leadership works at the individual, team and organizational levels. Most importantly, this analysis must recognize that leadership is interconnected across disciplines and functions.

Recently, while working with a client, I asked a question about the leadership development and learning goals for a group of senior vice presidents. As they all had been identified as leaders by their organization, I was curious as to how they kept on top of their leadership game – which competencies they were good at and which needed to be worked on or added to their skill sets.

In the main, most of the vice presidents I asked this question to had not intentionally marked out what their leadership requirements were. Neither had they considered a leadership development plan for themselves. I suggested that if there was no clear path for improving leadership across the board, how would they know how BRAVE or courageous they were being as leaders?

I am conscious that for some people the concept of having to set out a leadership development plan across the organization can be a bit of a challenge. I am also aware that working with different cultures and expectations across the leadership pipeline can give different results. However, I think that to act as BRAVE leaders, we must be really clear about our objectives for leadership. We must provide clear guidelines as to what systemic leadership looks like across the organization and, in particular, make sure that it is inclusive. It is important to be very intentional in creating a leadership system and looking at the skills needed to maintain it, looking at the impact it has across the organization for all stakeholders, and being able to test it to see if it is robust and fit for purpose.

There is no one right way to create an inclusive leadership system, and the variables will differ from organization to organization. However, thinking about this offers an ideal opportunity for leaders like you to be able to sit down and think about how to create and maintain a system that is specific to your ways of working.

Throughout this book, I refer to systemic leadership and the things that will help to develop this. And in thinking about building such a system, I look at strategic thinking, how to make BRAVE and courageous decisions and what it means to lead by example. And I explore the relevance of coaching in the organization along with many other ways to make this system quite robust. The idea is not to create some kind of silver bullet or a list of things that you need to tick off, but rather to expand your mind and allow you to start thinking more widely and more deeply about how inclusive leadership systems can work for your organization.

Chapter 3

Courageous decision-making

Imagine for a moment that you are the leader of a team or a senior manager or executive – the head of country even – and the ball lands at your feet, meaning that you have to make a crucial decision. It might be about:

- reporting bad news to the press;
- restructuring the company and making redundancies;
- cutting back on overheads on learning and development; or
- changing policy around working from home.

When you face those demands, what decision models are you drawing from? What decision models are those around you drawing from?

In fact, I should ask first whether you have you ever been taught or coached how to make decisions or shown what models are available.

At the heart of my approach around inclusive and BRAVE leadership is helping leaders make sense of the world around them, make better decisions and take appropriate action. I get my clients to consider that it's OK that their first reaction or response to a situation won't necessarily solve the issue. I want them to see that decision-making is an iterative process.

I am fully conscious that it is easy to say this as a coach, operating at a hundred feet above and looking at the bigger picture of the organization. Exploring the system rather than being dragged into the day-to-day minutiae of how an organization runs or, being really honest, the emotional baggage that comes from being part of any one of my clients' operations. This means it can be easy to skip over the questions, thoughts or assumptions that are running through clients' minds when they are navigating change. They may be thinking:

- What impact will this whole process have on my actual job?
- If I say the wrong thing, what are the chances of being sued or losing income?
- My risk appetite is low. I have a mortgage and three kids in private school. If I speak my truth, will this then end up on social media or Glassdoor?
- Will my competitors, and existing clients, seize on the situation if I do make a mistake?
- If it does go wrong, will people view me as an imposter?

Variations of these questions, and more, are often posed to me as a coach. This is when you get to see people at their most vulnerable – professionally – and there is a duty of care to ensure that these concerns are explored truthfully but with empathy and compassion.

My client was worried about the reputation of his organization. As the CEO of a relatively young and rapidly growing company, he was concerned about how the brand was perceived internally and externally. He was seeing that people who had left the company were writing on sites like Glassdoor about their not so positive experiences there, and there were also internal conversations about race and gender representation in the senior executive and management roles.

As someone who was used to just having a chat with colleagues – junior as well as more senior people in the company – over a beer or a coffee if things went a bit wrong, this was new territory.

How was it that people who would once come and talk to him any time they wanted to were now feeling that they couldn't? What options were available to him to be able to make changes?

Then came the stream of demands. He caught wind, before the staff conference, of the fact that staff were going to ask some difficult questions in the Q&A session.

How would he be able to answer these questions? Should he answer them?

Could they be passed on to another member of the senior management team? How would that look?

For many of the leaders in organizations I have worked with from 2019 onwards, internal and external organizational challenges have been exaggerated by the COVID-19 pandemic, the racial awakening following the murder of George Floyd and the economic challenge of people working from home.

How the hell were they to manage or lead in a situation none of us have experienced before?

My services as a speaker were in demand as all of this unfolded, as people sought ways to navigate the changing world. But when I scratched beneath the surface, what people really wanted was some form of coaching. I was thrown in at the deep end, and this period really tested my skills as a coach and facilitator. but I knew I had the coaching tools, coaching supervision, a good business mentor and my network to help me navigate this new terrain. The question was what was the best way to offer assistance?

Given this backdrop, the remainder of this chapter focuses on how leaders can employ the BRAVE model when making decisions and solving problems.

BRAVE decision-making

There are lots of tools you can draw on for decision-making. Here, I explore a few of the ones I recommend more commonly and show how we, as inclusive leaders, can use them.

The rational decision-making model

The rational decision-making model involves a systematic process of gathering information, evaluating alternatives and choosing the best option based on logical reasoning. The steps include:

1. identifying the problem;
2. gathering information relevant to the problem;
3. identifying alternative solutions;
4. evaluating each alternative, based on criteria such as feasibility, effectiveness and cost;
5. choosing the best option based on the evaluation;
6. implementing the chosen solution; and
7. evaluating the outcome and making adjustments if necessary.

The rational decision-making model is often used in business settings, where decisions need to be based on objective data and analysis.

The behavioural decision-making model

The behavioural decision-making model takes into account the psychological and emotional factors that can influence decision-making. This model recognizes that people often make decisions based on intuition, emotions and personal biases. The steps in this model include:

1. recognizing the problem;
2. identifying the emotions and biases that may be influencing the decision;
3. considering alternative solutions;
4. evaluating options based on how they align with your personal values and emotions;
5. making a decision based on a balance of logical reasoning and emotional factors; and
6. evaluating the outcome and reflecting on the decision-making process.

The behavioural decision-making model is often used in situations where personal values and emotions play a significant role.

The intuitive decision-making model

The intuitive decision-making model is based on the idea that people sometimes make decisions based on instinct or intuition, without consciously considering alternatives or weighing up the pros and cons. This model often applies in situations where time is limited or information is incomplete. This involves:

1. recognizing the problem;
2. making a decision based on instinct or intuition that draws on past experiences and knowledge; and
3. evaluating the outcome and reflecting on the decision-making process.

While the intuitive decision-making model can be useful in certain situations, it is important to note that relying solely on intuition can lead to bias and errors in judgement.

So, rather than rely solely on intuition, if you follow a structured process (as in the rational and behavioural models) you can make better decisions that lead to more positive outcomes.

The Cynefin framework

The Cynefin framework[5] is a decision-making model that helps individuals and organizations make sense of complex or uncertain situations. It consists of five domains – clear, complicated, complex, chaotic and disorder – and emphasizes the importance of understanding the nature of a situation in order to determine the appropriate course of action across the five domains.

- In the *clear* domain, the situation is clear and the appropriate course of action is obvious.
- In the *complicated* domain, the situation is complex and requires analysis and expertise to determine the appropriate course of action.
- In the *complex* domain, the situation is unpredictable and requires experimentation and adaptation to determine the appropriate course of action.
- In the *chaotic* domain, the situation is unstable and requires immediate action to steady the situation.
- In the *disorder* domain, the situation is unclear and further analysis is needed to determine which of the other domains is appropriate.

Often in my coaching I realize clients don't know these models and frameworks are available to them. A whole other book could be written to break down how different models

---

[5] See The Cynefin Co, 'The Cynefin framework'. Available from: https://thecynefin.co/about-us/about-cynefin-framework/ [accessed 24 September 2023].

can be applied to specific situations. The key things to note about the range of models is that whichever you choose, you should aim for alignment with personal and organizational values, consensus and often speed when making decisions. They should enable you to have the courage to be Bold, Resilient, Agile, Visionary and Ethical.

As a leader, you should at least be aware of what models exist, and if you are not sure how to apply them, then seek some kind of learning or guidance to help you see which ones are best for you when making different sorts of decisions.

There is a temptation to replicate the ways other organizations – often very large organizations, such as Amazon – apply decision-making models. But real courage is working out what aligns best with your specific circumstances rather than trying to follow a 'cookie cutter' approach.

Readers who have a bit more experience with decision-making models may have noticed I haven't included the Vroom-Yetton-Jago model or the recognition-primed decision model.[6] Well spotted, but the emphasis here is on recognizing what your specific needs are rather than me telling you which models to use.

Let's go back a bit to the BRAVE model.

- Is your decision-making Bold?
- Are the models you use Resilient? Can they withstand critique, or economic, social or political headwinds?
- Are they Agile and flexible enough to change if needs be?
- Are they Visionary in the sense of being aligned with the vision of your team, department or organization?

---

[6] The original Vroom-Yetton model was set out in V. Vroom and P. Yetton, *Leadership and Decision Making* (1973), and this was added to later by Jago; see V. Vroom and A.G. Jago, *The New Leadership* (1988). The recognition-primed decision model is discussed in G. Klein, *Sources of Power: How People Make Decisions* (1998).

- Are they Ethical and sustainable?

The BRAVE model is not a checklist, but rather a guide to the things you need to take into consideration as you navigate your leadership role. I often wonder how many organizations could have saved themselves a lot of trouble and money if they had used this approach.

If you go back and look at the sorts of questions that can land at the feet of someone in a position of leadership in an organization, you will realize that decision-making is never straightforward or easy.

Imagine that your company's revenue is down substantially. The hires you made the year before, betting that the market would expand and grow, have bloated your salary expenditures. The board have come back after conversations with investors and other stakeholders to say redundancies have to be made.

You sit there for a minute, thinking of the friendships you have made with colleagues. You may have shared experiences with them, had photos taken together and even shared secrets with them, and now you have to look them squarely in the eye (or not) and tell them that unfortunately, due to circumstances outside your control, you have to let them go. And you have to do this knowing that not long ago they were looking for a salary increase or sharing how tough things were at home.

This is the reality of leadership. Tough and often painful decisions have to be made for the organization, and this will affect individuals. Heck, you might even be sat there wondering if your own financial future is at stake too.

Problem-solving for leaders

Now let's move on to the issue of problem-solving.

Hands up if you were ever trained or coached on how to solve a problem. What methods were you taught? Were you able to pass learnings on to others?

There are times when I look at innovative companies like Dyson, Tesla, Patagonia, Netflix or Apple. I consider how they viewed the markets they were in and what they did to tear up the rule books so that they could see the problems that existed in their industries through a different lens.

It is fascinating to see how these companies looked at the existing products, or the approaches that were historically taken, and decided that they were going to flip the script and do something totally different, like:

- rethinking the science of vacuum cleaning and producing cleaners without bags, as they do at Dyson;
- rethinking the way that cars could be powered by focusing on electricity instead of combustion, as they do at Tesla;
- rethinking how to reduce waste when producing outdoor clothing, and at the same time developing a company ethos that prioritizes preservation of the outdoors, as they do at Patagonia;
- rethinking the video hire industry and subsequently becoming a subscription video on-demand service as well as a production house, as they do at Netflix; and
- rethinking how phones can be used and building an ecosystem to support the phone together with other products, as they do at Apple.

This kind of thinking doesn't come about by accident, and of course a certain amount of planning was required to get the timing and marketing right so that these companies could gain market share and a competitive advantage long before others copied their models. But it is the problem-solving approach I want to focus on here.

As I mentioned in Chapter 2, I look at leadership through a systemic lens. Rather than the behaviours of just one or a few charismatic and persuasive characters, I tend to look at the kind of leadership thinking that is supported and fostered across the whole organization, and how this is reflected across all areas of the business, whether it be product development, marketing, finance, talent management, customer experience or any other function. Specifically, I see if I can identify BRAVE, courageous and inclusive leadership in that organization.

Imagine for a moment you are developing a product in the financial markets. Here, in the UK, I work with a number of clients across banking and insurance, and there are strict regulations around compliance. My clients know that it doesn't take much for a mistake to be picked up on. And they know that the impact of that can be devastating. For instance, the company might be fined or its key market may lose confidence in it.

When coaching clients through the product development process, I often identify a whole array of problems that can arise around the product cycle. Individuals get an opportunity to list all the potential problems they can think of. Often they raise an objection to the way a product is currently being developed, and this can cause a bit of anxiety, especially if a junior member disagrees with, say, a senior developer. But I encourage them to raise the point anyway. Focus on the *problem* rather than the *person*.

People run free with the number of issues that can hinder progress in developing products. These can be around accessibility, colour scheme, sustainability, cultural implications, technologies used, design thinking and so many more. I throw these problems out as questions to be answered.

Very often leaders are expected to have all the answers. Either they put this expectation on themselves or they have direct reports or other colleagues who think this should be the case.

Surely if you are the chief information officer, you should have all the information, right?

If you are the country manager, then surely you are the go-to resource for all things we need to know about that country, right?

If you are the fire warden, then you should be aware of every eventuality should there be a fire, or you should know what to do during a fire drill if a pathway is blocked, right?

The reality is that this expectation is misplaced. The assumption that a leader is some kind of oracle that we should place on a pedestal is one of the things that can really hinder progress when trying to solve complex issues. Rather, there is something incredibly courageous about leaders who make it clear that it is not their role to fix everything but they can use their experience and intellect to help point people in the right direction to solve problems themselves. And in some cases it is the rallying of other minds around them that can help the leader to solve a problem.

At this point, I introduce some different tools that we can use for problem-solving. I want to explore some of the thinking behind problem-solving and the specific practical tools that can be used by BRAVE leaders to solve problems.

Thinking about problem-solving

Let's have a look at two different kinds of thinking when it comes to problem-solving: one is convergent thinking and the other is divergent thinking.

Convergent thinking is a thought process or method used to narrow down a set of ideas to find the best solution to a problem. It involves analysing and evaluating different options and selecting the one that is most feasible or practical.

Divergent thinking is a thought process or method used to generate a wide range of ideas without necessarily judging their feasibility or practicality. It involves exploring different possibilities and brainstorming creative solutions to a problem.

Tools for problem-solving

There are a number of problem-solving tools available to leaders, and the use of each will depend on the problem and the organizational context. These include first principles thinking, affinity mapping, and failure mode and effects analysis. But here I highlight the two I tend to use most in the work I do around inclusive leadership. These are the five 'w's approach and SWOT analysis.

The five 'w's approach

This is useful for defining the problem and then exploring what data or analysis is required to solve the problem. Five core 'w' questions are posed: What? Where? When? Who? Why?

What? – This question examines the nature of the problem and the resources available to solve it. Start off by asking:

- What is the issue here?

You can then follow up with a series of other questions that help to explore the problem, such as:

- What do we all need to know about this issue?
- What is an ideal scenario for solving the problem?
- What tools or metrics will we use to assess the problem?
- What resources do we have internally or externally to help solve this?

You continue to drill down, using more 'what' questions, to get as clear a picture as possible of the problem.

Where? – This series of questions identifies the precise place or location associated with the problem.

- Where does the problem typically generate from?
- Where might we expect similar issues to crop up?

When? – These questions can be used to examine when the problem first occurred and to identify a specific deadline for solving the problem.

- When was the problem first noticed?
- When does the problem need to be fixed?
- When will we implement a solution?

Who? – These questions explore who the stakeholders are and who could be affected by the problem.

- Who is affected by the problem?
- Who are the key stakeholders involved in the process?
- Who is the owner of this problem?
- Who will decide if we have solved the problem?

Why? – These questions explore the reason for the situation.

- Why do we need to solve the problem?
- Why is this happening to begin with?

The 'why' questions get to the underlying causes of the problem, or the contributing factors. It is a form of root cause analysis. It is recommended that leaders ask the 'why' question five times. A bit like we did when we were kids looking for answers to problems – or just being annoying! This is often referred to as the 'five whys'. The aim is to find causes of the problem, not identify symptoms.

SWOT analysis

The main objective of this tool is to allow people in organizations, mainly those in positions of leadership, to look at a specific problem and analyse that problem based on the four pillars of the SWOT tool: strengths, weakness, opportunities and threats.

Strengths and weaknesses focus on the *internal* resources which are readily available to you. These can be financial resources, human resources, existing processes and physical resources like premises and equipment.

Strengths are those factors you have that play to a unique position or competitive advantage. For example, if your organization is well funded, that can contribute to long-term decisions about investment or marketing.

Weaknesses are those factors that may cause a disadvantage around decision-making and problem-solving. For example, if you don't have enough employees for a project that you want to compete on, that amounts to a weakness.

Opportunities and threats, on the other hand, tend to focus on *external* factors and resources currently outside your control. These relate to market trends, the economy, the political landscape, economic regulations, demographic trends and so on.

If there is a new advancement in, say, AI (artificial intelligence) technology, or cheaper access to finance, this can serve as an opportunity that can help with decision-making.

By the same token, factors such as high interest rates, new legislation or changes in the way that your country trades with other countries (as was the case with Brexit) can be threats that hinder good decision-making.

SWOT analysis helps develop awareness of the factors that need to be considered when making decisions, whether these are to do with exploring new market opportunities, focusing on growth in existing markets, engaging in diversity and inclusion initiatives or exploring product development opportunities.

Like any tools used in organizational decision-making, the five 'w's and SWOT analysis have limitations around how objective the results can be, but they are a starting point for leaders looking to make decisions and solve problems.

Why is this important for BRAVE leaders?

These tools encourage you, as a leader, to consider options, and this can help you to make courageous decisions.

I am conscious that the way you work in your specific business, sector, industry or community will be shaped by location, policies and processes, among other factors. My intention is never to underplay the impact of those pressures or pretend those unique circumstances don't impact the way you make decisions. Rather, I aim to show that if you can leave space to think and consider what your options are, you will make better decisions.

The tools shared here are subject to the personalities, egos (including your own) and varying worldviews of the people you work with. Putting theory into practice is a whole other issue altogether, but I aim to offer you some guidance about how to implement a BRAVE mindset as part of your leadership.

The key thing to remember is that once you are equipped with useful tools, you can think about how BRAVE and inclusive your decision-making and leadership is. Can you make BRAVE decisions and, if so, is this something other leaders you work with can do as well?

Being BRAVE requires a certain mindset as well as access to tools and strategies to help you make the appropriate business case and build scenarios to win over people to your way of thinking.

In the next chapter, I move beyond problem-solving to explore the importance of strategic thinking for BRAVE leaders.

Chapter 4

Strategic thinking as a practice

When I first started working on how to make leadership more inclusive, there were a number of people who scoffed at the idea. It was dismissed by organizations who thought it would be nice to be more inclusive for publicity reasons, if they were ever questioned about diversity, but this was not something that was taken seriously.

Some people thought this idea was too liberal and nothing to do with the fundamentals of running a business. There were those who saw inclusion as just about ticking boxes for gender, class and ethnicity. More recently, some associated it with the trend towards environmental, social and corporate governance. But, generally, the thinking was: if it can't be tied to specific financial metrics, then what is the point of being more inclusive?

I am constantly testing out the thinking, and efficacy, of the BRAVE model that underpins my work. The reality of leadership development in organizations is a lot more brutal and ugly than most people make it out to be, so I want to make sure that my model is more than some kind of ideal to aspire to.

Despite the idealism we see around leadership – in the nice memes some people like to post, for instance – people still get sacked unfairly, products still get designed without considering how certain groups, like women, use them and people still don't know how to manage conflict properly. Leadership is messy. Because of this, I wanted to ensure that the BRAVE model was locked into some kind of thinking that could be tested and tweaked and that would hold up under scrutiny. In sum, I wanted it to be strategic.

In 2013, I met a gentleman at a leadership conference. He had just moved from being the diversity and inclusion manager at a media company to a new role in Big Four consultancy. We spoke about how he navigated resistance. A white, gay, disabled man, he spoke of not only his privileges but also the disadvantages he faced. In our conversation, he told me that while his remit was about improving diversity in the company, gender – not disability – was the organization's main focus. The thinking in the organization was that once it figured out how to handle gender diversity, then everything else would fall into place.

When he told me that, my initial thought was 'what the heck?' My language was a bit stronger but that was the sentiment.

What kind of tomfoolery was going on? How could this company hire someone as an expert to help shape their diversity strategy while at the same time marginalizing that same individual? Couldn't they see the irony of it all?

They really missed a beat on how they could have been more inclusive. They could have tapped into the learnings from this employee's lived experience both to make a difference within their talent pool and to understand parts of their customer base. That is some kind of crazy!

It fired up in me a real desire to speak unfiltered on inclusive leadership.

I went away and researched companies who had worked on inclusivity, but every single time the focus came back to strategies to increase talent diversity. But for me, inclusive leadership was so much more than just talent management. I wanted to know how it impacted product design, customer service, supply chain relationships, board selection, internal and external communications and any other area of business where processes might be impacted by lack of understanding of marginalization.

In the autumn of 2019, I had a pivotal conversation with a client. Two members of the diversity and inclusion team at a global hospitality brand approached me to see if I could work with them. They were concerned about how to tackle increasing problems around gender and racial prejudice across management. I made it clear I would happily come in to do some coaching through a leadership lens.

My idea was that framing the issues through the lens of systemic leadership would help to make people accountable for their decisions and their behaviours. I had seen more than my fair share of organizations taking umbrage with leaders who tried to impose values of inclusion on staff, or managers being confronted by their peers as misogynistic or racist. So I knew from the jump that there would be resistance if we didn't frame these issues through this lens.

These conversations really spurred on my thinking about how I could continue to both evangelize about inclusive leadership and its impact on the workforce and shape the practical application of my work. But I was to be truly tested by two key moments in 2020.

The first was the global pandemic. I had just got back from a family holiday in Morocco in February 2020 when the warnings started that the country was possibly going to go into a lockdown. I can honestly say that I was very nervous about what was going to happen to my business since, in the main, my work was delivering face-to-face presentations, facilitation or coaching services.

But I found I still had people's attention. Perhaps more so since there was nowhere for them to go. Zoom, Google Meet and Microsoft Teams were the places where people were getting together. We were in the 'never before' and had no option other than to sit down and listen to each other from the comfort or discomfort of our homes.

The second major event was the killing of George Floyd in Minnesota in May 2020, which sparked anti-racism protests and had widespread coverage in the media. With most people in the UK, Europe and the US working from home, our professional and personal timelines on both social and mass media were full of both this story and the killings of two other African Americans, Breonna Taylor and Ahmaud Arbery.

A global conversation started on the death of Black people at the hands of the police, driven mainly by the political and social movement Black Lives Matter. A slew of organizations realized that they had many disgruntled employees who were speaking out about their own experiences of marginalization at work. Unfair recruitment practices, lack of promotion and inappropriate language and behaviour were front and centre in these conversations.

On 31 May 2020, I recorded, edited and published a video called *Centring Black Lives*. In this video, I wanted to put together my thoughts and verbalize the trauma Black professionals across the Western world were feeling. This video was a resource not only for those in my network who had been asking me questions they were too afraid to ask in public, but also for the wider business community I was part of. It provides an honest and forthright narrative from several of us who have experienced racial bias and racism in our working lives.

If I thought my phone and inbox were busy in March, I was about to see that increase tenfold.

George Floyd's death had sparked a panic for global firms as they looked to address the conversation around racial inequity. And in the summer of 2020, my inbox filled up with requests from companies looking to have someone speak on how they could navigate workplace dissatisfaction related to racial discrimination.

These requests came in as leaders were already struggling with how with how to navigate the 'black swan event' that was COVID-19 and the global lockdown that followed. Organizations were put into a corner, not knowing how to navigate these new spaces and conditions. The ensuing crisis management was incredibly new for leaders who were used to times of prosperity and growth and had no kind of preparation, coaching or training for the likes of these events, which were happening at a rapid pace.

As companies and professionals started to make enquiries about my speaking and training, I was at pains to explain that my main area of focus was around inclusive leadership and culture. I was not a race expert. I was not a diversity, equality and inclusion practitioner. For sure I could explain and give narratives of the lived experience of myself and others, but the context of my work was much wider. Regardless, the enquiries kept on coming, and it turned out to be a far a busier year than I had expected.

I would regularly have conversations with clients along the lines of:

'David, we have had a major problem over the last couple years.'

'Go on.'

'As proud as we are of having recruited from a very diverse base of candidates, we realize that by the time these graduates are in the second or third year of working with us, they quit.'

'This is not peculiar to your firm, but do go on.'

'Well, we had a major and visible exodus of Black professionals from the firm a while back, and this incident in 2020 has highlighted the need for us to address this.'

'Address what exactly?'

'Do I have to spell it out?'

'Well, I don't want to read into something with my own assumptions and biases, so it would be better if you did.'

And so started several similar conversations I had with people who made enquiries about how I could help them as a speaker and a coach. These enquiries ranged across banking, tech, media, insurance, law, hospitality, food and beverages, fashion and a host of other verticals.

I asked questions, dug deep into the assumptions they made about me and challenged the assumptions I made about them. After all, that is what a coach does, right?

What a lot of organizations had ignored up until this point was how people from different racial and ethnic backgrounds were being marginalized by leadership and how this cascaded through the company. I wanted leaders to really sit in that discomfort and see how it showed up in this specific area, but more importantly I wanted them to look at the whole landscape of inclusion as part of their leadership DNA.

Was inclusion an issue in other areas of the business? In salary, gender, supply chain choices, customer service, age, ability, sexual orientation, product development?

For me, race and ethnicity was just a jumping off point for leaders to interrogate the impact of their leadership.

As leaders jumped onto calls with me, I sensed a need by many to find a silver bullet. They wanted me to provide quick answers to the problems that lay ahead of them. I was quick to advise that I don't do quick answers. I felt it was important to roll it back a bit first and see how problems could be solved through strategic thinking. I wanted to make sure the solutions were the right ones, rather than rushed responses.

What is strategic thinking?

This is a question that has kept coming up with clients over the years.

I don't want to be salty to those who have MBAs or who are in senior positions of leadership yet still don't quite get what I am talking about, so I spend some time explaining what strategic thinking is and why, for me, it is a key component of inclusive leadership.

At its most basic, strategic thinking focuses on finding and developing unique opportunities to create value for your organization. It is a way of leveraging both internal and external resources to reach a goal.

Strategic thinking refers to the cognitive process of analysing complex situations, identifying opportunities and challenges, and formulating effective plans and actions to achieve long-term goals. It involves the ability to think critically, anticipate future trends and make informed decisions that align with the overall vision and objectives of an organization.

It is one thing to think of this academically, to apply it in a perfect world, but a whole other thing to practise it in the real world. Just before I explore its practical application, I want to share some key characteristics of strategic thinking.

Key characteristics of strategic thinking

It is important for me to nerd out for a minute and explain some concepts so I can tie them back to being BRAVE.

Strategic thinking involves viewing the organization as a complex system with interconnected parts. It requires those doing the thinking to understand the relationships, dependencies and dynamics among various internal and external factors that impact an organization. By considering the broader context, strategic thinkers can identify potential impacts and make more informed decisions.

This thinking focuses on the future rather than merely reacting to current circumstances. It involves envisioning possible scenarios and anticipating changes, trends and emerging opportunities or threats to the organization, or units within the organization. Strategic thinkers proactively plan and position the organization for long-term success, which can seem a bit counterproductive when you are tasked with decision-making in the here and now, but walk with me...

Strategic thinking requires leaders to possess strong analytical and critical thinking skills. You gather and analyse relevant information, assess risks and uncertainties, and evaluate multiple options. You identify patterns, connections and insights to inform your decision-making process.

It involves generating creative ideas and exploring innovative approaches to problem-solving. It requires thinking beyond traditional solutions and considering new perspectives. It requires you to embrace experimentation and encourage a culture of innovation within your organization. For want of a better corporate cliché, it requires thinking outside of the box. Strategic thinking may not always sit well with others.

It is important that decisions and actions are aligned with the genuine overall vision, mission and goals of the organization, rather than some PR version. Often leaders forget this, but you have to take into account your organization's values, purpose and strategic direction in every decision-making process. This, at its most basic level, has to be the jumping off point, because this not only helps you and other leaders understand how your decisions contribute to a larger framework, but also shapes how you share communicate the organization's values to others.

What is the point of being BRAVE in isolation or without buy-in? How do you build trust if you can't demonstrate why this is important? Why the heck are we talking about future planning when we have issues to solve right here and right now?

And this is where I share that another characteristic of strategic thinking is focusing on being Agile in response to changing circumstances. Given that Agile is one of the pillars of the BRAVE model, this is a way to embed that learning too. This agility helps leaders anticipate potential challenges, adjust plans as needed and be open to feedback and course corrections. Leaders too must understand the importance of continuous learning and improvement for achieving strategic objectives.

You see, strategic thinking allows leaders to make informed decisions based on careful evaluation and analysis. In weighing up the pros and cons, considering multiple alternatives and assessing potential outcomes and consequences, leaders can make decisions that align with the organization's goals and values.

Several potential clients came to me after I said that putting up black squares on social media and promising to do better was not a strategic way of showing representation and understanding. If this is all you do, you will be called out and have your values and integrity challenged. Much like organizations who have put out comments in the press and social media in support of equal pay on the basis of gender when there is unequal treatment within their own ranks.

For strategic thinking to work, it takes patience. It takes additional bravery to do this through the lens of inclusion too. If it were easy, everyone would be doing it, right?

Importance of strategic thinking

Now I have clarified what the necessary components are for strategic thinking, I want to explore why it is so important. Again, if I am stating the obvious, I prefer to do so to make the point clear.

It is important to think strategically, especially if you want a healthy and sustainable organization. The ability to anticipate and prepare for the future by considering potential opportunities and challenges allows you to proactively shape your organizational or departmental trajectory, respond to emerging trends and have more informed and effective decision-making.

By identifying unique opportunities and being clear on positioning, strategic thinking can offer a competitive advantage. It allows organizations to differentiate themselves in the market. Why wouldn't anyone want to include this as part of their overall thinking?

Going deeper on this, you could add resource optimization and focus on how you as the leader prioritize initiatives, allocate budgets and align actions with values. Then there is employee engagement and alignment with values in customer experience journeys, product development roadmaps and so much more, which all add to up to why strategic thinking is important.

But there are still so many organizations across the private, public and third sectors, small and large, that still won't take into consideration the importance of strategic thinking and how it ultimately leads to better decisions. We see time and time again rash decision-making and poorly thought-out execution. 'Act in haste, repent at leisure' might seem like a cliché but many leaders have become unstuck just because they haven't thought things through with the longer term in mind.

My aim is to leave you with no excuse not to think strategically. Now you know better, you will do better.

Next, let's explore how strategic thinking ties into inclusive leadership.

Strategic thinking for inclusive leadership

Inclusive leadership at its heart emphasizes creating an environment where diverse voices and perspectives are heard, valued and considered when making decisions. Strategic thinking involves the ability to analyse complex situations, anticipate challenges and develop effective long-term plans. How, then, do we understand the vital relationship between the two and highlight the benefits of integrating these two concepts?

In today's rapidly changing and diverse business landscape, people can be hard-pressed to take the time out even to consider ideas like inclusive leadership and strategic thinking. As I write this, I think of organizations who ignored strategic thinking and made decisions that they later had to roll back – maybe to do with pay scales or working practices.

Of course, organizations are not static. Leaders are always going to have to make choices around what is a priority, be it staffing, marketing, workplace policies. And impact in the wider community will always shift according to the latest social, economic and political temperature.

In Chapter 1, I spoke about the principles underlying inclusive leadership. I have since spoken about how those benefits can enhance organizational performance. But it is also important at this juncture to recognize that there are challenges and barriers to introducing and implementing inclusive leadership.

Biases and historic ways of working will always rear their ugly heads. This is how we are as humans. We default to heuristics and ways of seeing the world that protect us and make us feel safe. Whether we are in the savannah or the urban jungle, this is how we do it.

If recruiting from the same kind of university or the same demographic has worked, then why on earth would someone thrust into a position of leadership want to stick their neck out and test that theory?

Unless you are shown the relevance of your own blind spots and areas that can be improved on, why would you want to change?

In addition, there will be gaps in knowledge and skills to effectively implement inclusive leadership practices. I have lost count of the number of times leaders have rolled their eyes when they hear that they have mandatory unconscious bias training. For the record, I am not a fan of this myself, as I believe we have a host of conscious biases we need to navigate first... but I digress.

If there is a lack of diversity among leaders, especially at senior levels, this can perpetuate homogeneous decision-making and hinder inclusive leadership. This is not to say a group who share the same gender, class or ethnic grouping cannot lead an organization or make good decisions. Rather, making room for difference and challenging group-think is a sure-fire way to improve decision-making. Breaking down barriers to diverse representation in leadership roles is essential to drive inclusive practices. Organizations that can implement strategies around recruitment and promotion processes, mentorship programmes and more robust evaluation systems can at least start on the path of building inclusive leadership into their organizational DNA.

This is not easy, though. Convincing people of a new way of thinking, decision-making and acting will take the same amount of effort, if not more, as implementing any new strategy.

Finally, without clear accountability measures, efforts may remain superficial or inconsistent. Establishing metrics, goals and regular assessments can hold leaders accountable for fostering inclusivity within their teams and across their organization.

Strategic thinking allows leaders to look at these principles on inclusive leadership and embed then into their long-term thinking.

To help clients marry these principles together, I usually ask a series of pointed questions:

- What does ideal leadership look like across the organization?
- What honestly needs to be in place for the leadership to be seen as inclusive?

- How do you foster an inclusive culture using strategic thinking?
- Do people understand inclusive leadership without you explaining it?
- What are the core principles that shape decision-making for you and others in leadership?

These questions, and others that leaders have posed, are not intended to elicit some glib response that just serves to make the person look better. Instead, the aim is to encourage well-thought-through answers. Answering these questions with full honesty requires a level of chutzpah. Change is never easy. Communicating a strategy and direction for your organization is not easy either.

The aim here is for leaders to see the connection between strategic thinking and inclusive leadership. Rather than seeing these as isolated ideas that should be left to specific individuals or departments, strategic thinking and inclusive leadership should be viewed as parts of the same approach to support everyone in working towards organizational goals.

This leads to the last point I want to make about strategic thinking as a practice. How should leaders approach strategic thinking and innovation?

Strategic thinking for innovation

Let's define innovation as the ability of an organization either to define, design and deliver new goods or services to customers or to build on and improve existing products or processes.

Innovation is important for any organization. It is tied into sustainability. It is part of a competitive advantage. It is a way of tapping into the creativity of your staff.

We have seen advances in the way we use phones, develop and track our fitness, diagnose illnesses and use AI. But at the same time, we realize that many of these innovations have only been developed with a small demographic in mind and are not very inclusive.

The author Caroline Criado Perez, in her award-winning book *Invisible Women*,[7] highlights the range of product and service areas that we take for granted but which were not designed with women in mind. From the size of smartphones to the efficacy of medication to the suitability of design for car safety (think of the positioning of seatbelts, headrests and airbags) – design without proper consideration for women is commonplace.

How can organizations truly call themselves innovative or strategic if a large part of their customer base is excluded or not considered in the design and final delivery of their products?

The challenge of the BRAVE leader and any organization looking to practise inclusive leadership is not only to flag those shortfalls and gaps but also to leverage strategic thinking and innovation to be more inclusive.

If you were the leader in product design, how comfortable would you be with confronting those areas where there is a shortage of inclusive thinking? Does the system of leadership you work in offer latitude and bandwidth for inclusion?

I am going to head right back to the BRAVE model to explore how this might be used around strategic thinking and innovation.

- *Bold* – When considering innovation, ask questions about the research being done around customers or other stakeholders. Use those questions as a means not to bamboozle or trip up others, but to embed innovation in the strategies of your organization. Don't be afraid of pushback. Prepare a strong case for your argument, and consider how to handle

---

[7] Caroline Criado Perez, *Invisible Women: Exposing Data Bias in a World Designed for Men* (2019).

the objections others may have. Get buy-in from collaborators who share the same view as you, and be transparent as to why your position on innovation and inclusion matters.

- *Resilient* – Demonstrate the case for managing risk in innovation. Get your staff to understand that resilience is a collective thing so that when exploring new ideas or developing old ones, the risk doesn't fall to one or two people but rather a number of people working together. Staff should have the courage to experiment with ideas but also know what risks come with being innovative – whether that risk is falling foul of regulations or upsetting customers used to old ways of doing business. Such risks should not bring about inaction but the ability to test things and also allow for those involved to remain strong if such innovation is rejected.

- *Agile* – This is an opportunity for flexibility, emotional strength and creativity when circumstances change, either internally or externally, for an organization. Advances in technology like generative AI can provide opportunities for organizations and the teams within them to see how quickly, effectively and sustainably they can adapt to these new technologies. Do these developments align with the strategy and can such advances cater for the needs of the stakeholders who will benefit from this innovation?

- *Visionary* – When considering innovation how does it align with Visionary leadership? There have been so many advances in industries in my lifetime. The smartphone, electric cars, GPS for travel – all these have changed the way many of us actually navigate our personal and professionals lives. The innovation it took to get here would have involved some courageous leaders dreaming big. Does your leadership make room for that kind of vision and larger thinking?

- *Ethical* – Sometimes people misunderstand what it takes to be ethical. Some simple questions that could be asked to give some guidance are: Is this sustainable? Is it just? Does the innovation we show have empathy for those who would benefit most from it?

The challenge to any leader is to be able to consider these things when making decisions. Being inclusive or thinking inclusively, especially when doing strategic thinking, is not easy but it is doable.

Now we understand a bit more about what strategic thinking is and how we can integrate strategic thinking and inclusive leadership, in the next chapter I explore how you can embed inclusive leadership across your team or organization.

Chapter 5

Mapping inclusion

In previous chapters, I walked you through the principles behind inclusive leadership. I looked at what it is and gained clarity around definitions and context for the purpose of this book. Then I explored why it is important by focusing on its importance for decision-making, problem-solving, strategic thinking and seeing leadership through the lens of the system rather than just the individuals who practise it.

Now I move to the 'how'. The implementation of this thinking that allows you to demonstrate what it means to be a BRAVE leader in your organization, or give guidance to those who wish to do the same. And I start by mapping inclusion across the organization.

When I deliver keynotes on inclusive leadership, I often share that a big part of winning hearts and minds to this approach is about where we start from. I totally understand why so many texts focus only on mapping talent or people. While I start there, this not the only space where I look at mapping inclusion.

Let's get to seeing what this mapping looks like across an organization. For the record, this is not a linear process – you are at liberty to map inclusion in any order you see fit.

Mapping inclusivity in talent journeys

Having had the privilege of working with several global clients across a variety of sectors on their talent programmes, I would like to suggest some ways that you can be a BRAVE leader by mapping how inclusive your employees' talent journeys are.

One of the first things that can be done in this process is to look at what is working already. Have a look at your marketing assets – your brochures, your social media and all the material that you use to get people to look into joining your company. You could look at where you advertize vacancies, what kind of universities or colleges you visit to attract talent, the spaces you find yourself networking in or the kinds of exhibitions and conferences that you go to in order to raise awareness of your specific brand.

In doing this kind of audit, you can get a sense of what you are already doing well, but it also gives you an opportunity to start thinking about blind spots or areas where you're not doing so well. And even if you're not sure about which areas you are doing less well in, this is an opportunity to work with stakeholders or other groups that can point out those blind spots for you.

Attracting talent

One of the things that strikes me when coaching large organizations around attracting talent is how keen they are to show they are racially diverse and have gender diversity as well. You can see this in their brochures and across their social media and other marketing assets.

The problem is that despite the inviting brochures, many individuals who come to these organizations from under-represented backgrounds – be it to do with race and ethnicity, class, disability and so on – come to realize that they are still outsiders. The brochures weren't good representations of what the organizations actually look like.

I have worked with clients to first find out how inclusive they really are and then identify practical means of improving on inclusion across the organization.

Whether the organization was recruiting locally or globally, the aim was that they would be a lot more considerate of the talent pools that they had missed out previously. For example, in the US, getting organizations to recognize that getting the best talent didn't have to mean only recruiting from Ivy League schools. Or in the UK, from Russell Group universities. I would also get them to think about where they could position themselves regionally or in career pro-grammes, or think about working with new recruitment partners.

For many leaders in talent management and recruitment, it requires a BRAVE act to let go of the idea that you only get the best from the top colleges and universities. This also applies to recruiters who always draw from the same talent pool of individuals who they consider to be the 'best' – indi-viduals who look, sound and even smell the same.

Imagine walking into a meeting with your leadership team, who all still believe that top business schools and uni-versities are the only source for good candidates, and telling them you are going to widen your reach and seek to attract people from institutions they have never heard of or never had any connection with?

One of my clients was based in Docklands, London. From one of their buildings, you got quite a panoramic view of the city. Not too far from this wealthy space that they occupied were boroughs experiencing extreme poverty. I was asked to come in to run a session on how they could expand their approach to attract talent from the surrounding areas into the business.

They already ran some good community outreach events where local students could find out more about the organization. But often when attendees would came forward, the only people with any level of seniority that they spoke to were middle-aged men and women who looked and sounded very different to them.

At one event, I planted some questions in the student audience to ask how the organization catered for people like them. What did career pathways look like? Were there others in the organization who had similar backgrounds? I told my client to be prepared for tough questions and to give honest responses.

One particular leader took a very BRAVE stance in front of the student audiences, saying they were very aware that the organization had not done enough to reach out locally. That they knew they would probably make some big mistakes along the way but that they were willing to take risks and try to make a difference.

I totally admired that stance but also stated to the client that this sort of BRAVE act should be systemic. It couldn't be left to one or two individuals to take this position while others just watch from the sidelines. This would mean that processes and systems would need to be put in place to make sure this leader's stance would be the rule and not the exception.

Changes to the way the organization was attracting talent would be difficult and would not create an easy win. And even with the best will in the world, if there was a restructure, a changing of the guard in terms of senior executives, or other demands made on the organization's culture, how could this intention to reach out more broadly be sustained?

BRAVE leadership is never easy or straightforward.

Hiring

The second stage of mapping talent to assess inclusivity considers the hiring process.

When leaders and organizations are equipped with the tools to hire inclusively, the spotlight is shone on the strengths and weaknesses of the current hiring process.

One area related to hiring that is explored in my client coaching is referrals. Some of the issues in the process of attracting talent, discussed in the previous section, come up here too.

Very often when I think of referral, it is about asking those who we lead to ask their friends and other individuals close to them whether they would be interested in job opportunities in the organization. The issue here is that people are more likely to refer others from the same background – let's face it, most of us would do this. The result is that we reach out to individuals who share the same characteristics as those already in the organization.

When I do talent referral with clients, I focus on them being deliberate around asking people to pick out those in their networks who do not necessarily fit the same mould as the existing talent in the organization. I want them to start to think differently about individuals who have different lived experiences, cultural experiences and even experiences related to class. I want them to see that these individuals could contribute in new ways that bring value to the organization and enhance innovation.

I really encourage clients to measure how wide and varied their techniques for attracting new talent into the organization are. The experience is different depending on the organization and the people, but when leaders look at how things are done in their organization, so many learn that they are able to extend their networks and their reach with just a few tweaks and just a bit more thinking about how to attract different kinds of talent from wider pools.

There are some easy ways to make hiring more geared towards inclusion. One way is to provide training on inclusive hiring for the individuals who work in talent and recruitment. For example, in interviews, rather than relying purely on subjective assessment of candidates, staff can be trained to apply more objective tools, such as a checklist covering competencies required for the position. Having your interviewers trained on how to build those lists and review them would be a bonus.

A second way is to explore how inclusive job descriptions are. The presence of certain words in the profile of a job description can determine whether or not individuals will choose to apply for the position. As with all these processes, it's important to be able to measure and see what works. You could compare the range of applicants attracted by differently worded adverts. Or you could ask those who applied for the job and were shortlisted why they decided to apply in the first place. (Obviously, it's not really feasible to find out why people decided not to apply.)

A third way is to make sure selection and interview panels are representative of different backgrounds. There is a lot of evidence to suggest that when hiring panels are made up of individuals with different experiences, they will look for different things in a candidate, and this helps to eliminate biases that would otherwise be present in the hiring process.

Managing performance

This leads me to the bit about inclusivity in performance management.

The Chartered Institute of Personnel and Development defines performance management as:

> the attempt to maximize the value that employees create. It aims to maintain and improve employees' performance in line with an organization's objectives. It's not a single activity, but rather a group of practices that should be approached holistically.[8]

---

[8] Chartered Institute of Personnel and Development, 'Performance management: An introduction' (2022). Available from: www.cipd. org/uk/knowledge/factsheets/performance-factsheet/ [accessed 24 September 2023].

Performance management is usually included as part of any employee's journey. In some organizations this can seem like this is a dark art, while in others it is a well-planned process of continuous feedback and regular reviews.

The challenge I find as a coach is getting leaders to explore how inclusive they are when doing those performance reviews. There have been several times where I have been called in to advise leaders on performance management only to find out that they have not been consistent or inclusive in their reviews. Often, this is because they are working with a system that doesn't give them agency to do this, though other times it's because they are not quite BRAVE enough.

A BRAVE leader could ask the following questions:

- How can I help you to do your best work?
- How can the organization help you to perform to your best ability?
- What part of your work would you want more responsibility on?
- What areas would you change?

Asking these questions might seem way too much for some leaders, but what's the harm in asking questions to try and get the best out of those you lead?

Very often it can be easy to assume that you know about everything that is going well. But in an increasingly global workforce where different demands are put on people, there is nothing wrong with asking how you might do better to make the person work more effectively and deliver better.

It is through these kinds of conversations that leaders can not only influence on-the-job performance, but also show consideration for some of the issues that individuals are experiencing outside of working hours. For example, I know of leaders who have taken this approach and realized that to cater for parents who are doing the school run, they should start meetings slightly later in the morning.

All of this is context driven. There needs to be an organizational culture that supports openness and the ability to have these conversations. Other than that, they are just good ideas that go nowhere. And what would be the point in that?

Very often, performance reviews can seem arbitrary. Or too often they can be seen just as part of a game that needs to be played to line people up for bonuses or pay raises. But they should do so much more than that. They are opportunities for collaboration. For sharing ideas. For mutual improvement of performance and growth.

Offboarding

No matter how good a leader you are (or think you are), there is going to be some part of the talent journey where either you must let the person go or they will decide to leave. Offboarding is the last part of the talent journey and a final opportunity to consider being inclusive.

There are several reasons why staff leave organizations. Maybe they feel that the organization just isn't a good fit for them any more, maybe there is a clash of personalities or expectations, or maybe they have been offered a better opportunity. Or, if things are really bad, they may just think the organization is trash and want to get the hell out of there.

What a BRAVE leader will aim for is a healthy exit. An opportunity to sit down and, as far as possible, ensure that all parties depart from the experience in good stead.

Much is written about inclusive onboarding and bringing new talent on, but just as important is inclusive offboarding, whether the person is leaving of their own choice or you are letting them go.

Offboarding and exit interviews are not easy to do. I mentioned before about maintaining regular contact with staff through the performance review process – this should mean that when you get to this place of exit, there will be less chance of nasty surprises.

Questions I have got leaders to ask at this point include:

- What did you enjoy most about working here?
- What did you enjoy least about working here?
- Are there any concerns or issues around working at this company you'd like to share?
- What advice would you give to new hires at the company?

Obviously this is a bit more difficult if you, as leader, have had to make a large swathe of people redundant or there is someone leaving under a cloud, but very often offboarding and an exit interview can be great ways to understand just how inclusive the talent journey has been for the person who is leaving.

Mapping customer experiences

When working with clients on the customer journey in organizations, I often like to start by getting them to be BRAVE in thinking about what this looks like for the customer.

If you are working in a small organization serving a niche market, this mapping of the customer journey probably won't need to be as comprehensive as if you are working in a large global organization. Nonetheless, the exercise is intended to increase awareness of customer experiences, the intention being to bolster your competitiveness and align with whatever USP or other advantage you already have.

Here are some questions to ask yourself as starting points:

- Do we have a process or map of the customer experience as it stands?
- What are the defining characteristics of our customer base?
- What is the process for onboarding clients?

- Is there also a process for offboarding clients?
- What feedback loops do we have in place to know how well we are doing with both?
- Do we know what we do well as part of the customer journey?
- What are our weaknesses around customer satisfaction and retention?

Sometimes, this can be done internally and a robust conversation comes out of it. Other times, it may require the intervention of facilitators and coaches like myself who aren't afraid to ask the hard questions and really challenge from the outside looking in.

The purpose of this exercise is to really get those who lead in the organization to think about the bits that are done well, but not ignoring the blind spots. The aim is to encourage leaders to be courageous enough to look at all eventualities. They might go online and view the sites that rate customer experience in whatever region they are, but they must not bristle at some of the negative comments – they should focus less on the person and more on the point being made.

If there are stark differences between the experiences of different customer groups, that tells you something about the inclusivity of your provision. This can lead you to consider how different groups are experiencing the customer journey and whether changes are needed to make certain aspects more accessible.

One client I worked with realized in the development of their service that no consideration had been given to those with restricted mobility. Historically, no consideration had been given to, for example, wheelchair users who may want to access their building.

Also, an increasing share of their customer base was people who did not have English as their first language, but no provision was made to offer translation of documents that were issued as part of their service. This kept on coming up in the customer feedback, so they had to sit down and think about how they could adapt their service accordingly to make sure all customers were catered for.

Getting this client to map customer experiences showed issues with physical access and access around language. This made them go back to the drawing board, though there were some in the organization who didn't think this was worthwhile. I had to demonstrate the commercial case for doing so. The questions I asked, such as those listed above (you will be able to come up with others), got the conversation started.

At this point you might be wondering whether this inclusive leadership is realistic. Is thinking about leadership through the lens of being BRAVE worth it? Does this expect us to be all things to all people?

Here's the thing. Inclusive leadership does not demand that from you by any measure. Rather, what mapping the customer experience does is get you to look to those areas that make the experience better for the people who are your customers. It allows you to stand out from the competition that has not considered these things. It makes those who provide customer support across the organization more attuned to how they can help your customers.

This is a marathon. Not a sprint.

You can't fix everything all the time, as the world is ever changing, but the process described here provides data that will show the things that matter to your customers and you can refer to this when you are able to give it your attention.

The Net Promoter Score (NPS)[9] is one tool that organizations use to measure customer experience. The NPS measures the loyalty of a company's customer base. It assigns a score from –100 to +100, which comes from customers answering the question: How likely are you to recommend this company to a friend or colleague?

How a customer answers this will be shaped by the experience they have. Asking some of the questions mentioned earlier can help you think about how the score can be improved.

Mapping customer experience journeys can show how inclusive they are in terms of the diverse needs, preferences and challenges of different customer segments. Based on this information, you can design experiences that cater to the unique requirements of your customers.

Here are some steps to help you map customer experience journeys:

- Identify and define customer segments.
- Consider demographics, psychographics, behaviour patterns and any other relevant factors.
- Group customers into segments that share similar characteristics or needs.
- Conduct research to gain a deeper understanding of each customer segment.
- Utilize methods such as surveys, interviews, focus groups and analytics to collect data.
- Pay attention to the diverse perspectives, experiences and preferences within each segment.
- Develop customer personas that represent the key characteristics and needs of each customer segment. These should capture information such as demographics, goals, challenges, motivations and preferred communication channels. Personas serve

---

[9] See Net Promoter System. Available from: www.netpromotersystem.com/about/benefits-of-net-promoter [accessed 20 November 2023].

as fictional representations of your customers and help you empathize with them.

Once you have taken the steps to map customer journeys in your organization, you can use the framework below to position customer experiences in stages from initial awareness to post-purchase loyalty:

1. awareness;
2. consideration;
3. purchase;
4. usage; and
5. loyalty.

You can customize the stages based on your specific organizational context. The key thing here is understanding that different customer segments may have their own paths and touchpoints at different stages. These include both digital and physical touchpoints – websites, social media, mobile apps, call centres, physical spaces and more. Consider how each touchpoint contributes to the overall experience.

When working with clients, I get leaders to analyse 'pain points' and opportunities. I ask them to look for potential barriers or challenges that specific customer segments might face. To consider accessibility, language preferences, cultural considerations and other factors that can impact inclusivity. The power is in the planning.

There is much to be said about designing inclusive customer experiences.

Mapping can help you create strategies and tactics that cater to the unique needs of different customer segments. This may involve personalization, targeted messaging, accessible design, language localization and cultural sensitivity.

I was working with a marketing company where the staff were mainly early-career twenty- and thirty-somethings. They were developing ads and content for an older market – people in their fifties and older. While they found it easy to use existing software for personalization and messaging for this age group, it was another thing to really be aware of localization and cultural sensitivity. This was not as easy as throwing a prompt into some AI software. The staff had to gather information from people in this age range, through surveys and focus groups, to understand some of the more nuanced approaches they would use in buying products or services.

There was resistance to this from some of the leadership team, but it was how we monitored the next stage that made a difference.

When the ads and content went live, we collected feedback from customers, tracked key performance indicators and used analytics to measure the impact these were having. At this point, commercial leaders would be looking at things like consumer acquisition cost or customer lifetime value and wondering if all the earlier efforts had been worth it.

Even so, by tracking impact, it is possible to make adjustments when necessary. Where possible, regularly review and refine your strategies based on data and customer insights and recognize that customer journeys are not static and will evolve over time. Gather feedback, conduct research and adapt your approach to meet changing customer needs and market trends and regularly update your inclusive customer experience strategies to stay relevant.

If you are going to be BRAVE, it's important to be methodical too.

These may sound like stating the obvious, but running exercises on customer journeys with teams across various disciplines has provided me with great insight into how companies are run as well as giving leaders opportunities to test their assumptions and build better customer service experiences.

Mapping product development

The last area I explore in relation to mapping to assess inclusion in your organization is product development.

One of my clients is a global food and beverage company. While this was a well-established firm, it had an unfortunate track record when it comes to talking about race at work, and this touched a bit of a raw nerve in 2020 when we had the racial awakening I discussed in Chapter 3, which shook a lot of Western corporations to the core. I was onboarded as a coach to facilitate conversations with the executive committee to tackle some of the sensitive issues around dealing with race. I knew I could walk them through these issues using a part of the BRAVE model I call 'BRAVE conversations'. It was important that they tackled this subject through the lens of inclusive leadership so that any course of action they decided on would be sustainable.

BRAVE conversations are based on four simple principles.

- *Love* – Start conversations, no matter how challenging, with the purpose that you are not there to belittle anyone, but rather to see how everyone can win. Don't start from the guilt of negative feelings but from the place where we centre the goodness of humanity.
- *Language* – Understand that there may be words and phrases that may mean different things to different people. Ask questions where you do not understand, and have the bandwidth to appreciate that just

because something means one thing to you, it doesn't mean that it can't mean something totally different to someone else. Context is important.

- *Listening* – Active listening is important where we are out to understand differing points of view. This doesn't mean that we all have to agree, but just as we make space for different meanings when we use particular terms, it is important to listen to understand people's perspectives. Instead of responding without thought, we can listen to get a sense of where the other person is coming from.

- *Leverage* – Once you have had conversations as a team using the love, language and listening pillars, you will be able to see what you have learned and what further questions you would love to have answered. Then you can consider how you might leverage that learning into something actionable.

I used this framework with this client to walk through some of the more challenging conversations that they had to have. After getting the feedback from the various sites (locations) we decided to have a leadership offsite to work through this feedback. At this point I would show them how inclusive leadership would look across their organization.

I drew a power/interest matrix at this meeting to emphasize what inclusion should look like across the organization. I asked them to think about all the touchpoints stakeholders came across in the organization and how these could make people feel that they were part of a two-way relationship.

Even if it was just a transactional touchpoint, how could it help stakeholders feel included?

What did inclusion look like at the different sites across the globe?

How could they take the learning from this contentious subject and apply this in a BRAVE way to other areas of the business?

These areas might include research on food preferences, supply chain choices in certain neighbourhoods and districts, and marketing campaigns. As well, given how regulated the food and beverage industry is, we explored how inclusive the organization was around finance and compliance decisions, considering whether regulations were viewed as a help or a hindrance. Were staff following them because they care about customers or just so they don't get sued?

Then, we explored how the answers to 'what' and 'why' questions that were part of this exercise could be interpreted to provide a different perspective on the ways of working and doing business. Rather than seeing inclusive leadership, and being BRAVE, just as something people were being forced into, I wanted them to consider how this approach could align with the values and culture they believed in.

The penny dropped.

One of the directors looked at me and said: 'I actually never saw it like that, Dave. Now it makes sense.'

~

It is moments like this that remind me why I do this work in the first place. The realization that there is a great business case for inclusive leadership. To be courageous and Resilient when people may see 'inclusion' as some kind of virtue signalling or political correctness or whatever pejorative du jour people adopt when we start talking about inclusion.

As part of my preparation for working with this client, I was able to nerd out on nutrition impacts across different cultures. I got to explore the role of epigenetics of consumers. I looked at how a range of their products aligned with the consumption habits and health concerns of people in South Asia compared to Europe, or North America compared to South America.

This simple exercise, which was first leveraged out of an uncomfortable conversation on how the executive team and other leaders in distribution could talk about race, was extended to other parts of the business. It allowed production to be seen through a different lens without the guilt of what may have gone wrong in the past hanging over the conversation.

There other popular examples of what happens when inclusion is at the heart of product development. Fenty Beauty, founded by the celebrity entrepreneur Rihanna, offers cosmetics in a wide range of skin tones. They include more ranges for women with darker skin than the standard offering and have become very profitable as a result, increasing the valuation of the brand and the company. Dove, Apple, Proctor and Gamble, Bumble, ASOS and a host of other companies have gone out of their way to be a lot more inclusive in product development, aiming to redress the balance for under-represented customers, be it around gender, ethnicity, age or a host of protected characteristics.

And yet there is much room for more BRAVE leaders to emerge.

In Chapter 4, when I was discussing strategic thinking, I spoke about the book *Invisible Women,* which highlights that so much about car design and safety doesn't take into consideration how women's bodies differ from men's in terms of muscle mass, bone density, spinal alignment and vertebrae and torso and limb form. Yet across the car industry there is no consensus on design that takes such differences into consideration, even though in most countries women drive as much as men.

I picked up some pointers from that experience with the food and beverage company around making product development inclusive.

One of my first tips would be to set clear design principles that prioritize inclusivity as a core value. These principles should guide the entire product development process – the focus should be on things like accessibility, usability representation and cultural sensitivity and a wide range of other user perspectives that good designers will recognize.

A second point would be to build teams that totally understand the importance of building inclusive products. These teams should come from varied backgrounds, with their own perspectives and skills, and they should be encouraged to collaborate and create an environment where they all feel valued and empowered to contribute their unique insights to improve product development. Those leading these teams should ensure that those insights are front and centre of any new product design or iteration on existing designs.

A third point would be to conduct user research and needs analysis that helps to make the product more inclusive. If you capture insights from potential users from different backgrounds and gain a deep understanding of your target audience and its diverse needs, preferences and challenges, it will definitely help towards building more inclusive products. Some of the examples I mentioned already, like Fenty and Dove, have done this to great advantage.

Some clients I have worked with have been willing to collaborate with external organizations, advocacy groups or individuals with expertise in accessibility and inclusivity. Being more inclusive doesn't just happen in-house; sometimes it requires stepping outside of your leadership bubble. Seeking partnerships that can provide guidance, insights and feedback on your product development, in addition to engaging diverse stakeholders throughout the development journey, can help in developing more inclusive products.

Finally, I would recommend you refine the product based on feedback. Actively listen to your user feedback and iterate the product design based on the insights gathered. In so doing, you can address usability issues, accessibility barriers or gaps in user needs. Continuously refine your product based on that feedback loop and prioritize inclusivity in every iteration.

I keep reminding you that this BRAVE work isn't easy.

If it was easy, then everyone would be doing it, but this book and the points I make in it can be the jumping off point to help you and your organization become more BRAVE around making the kinds of decisions discussed here.

More than talent

Although I deliberately started this chapter by focusing on talent, when it comes to mapping inclusion in an organization, I have shown that there is so much more to consider.

The principles involved in mapping inclusivity in talent experiences, customer experiences and product development can be applied to financial processes, procurement, innovation, marketing and other touchpoints within your organization.

The key is always to think about inclusivity in relation to the overall mission and objectives that are important to your organization. Alongside the commercial and business cases for running a business, there are cases to be made for cultural and ethical missions too.

The best way to understand inclusivity in your organization is to question things you are already doing and then look for gaps in knowledge and experience. As always, it takes courage to be able to challenge what already exists. I have provided ideas to help you to take that BRAVE leap as individuals, but more importantly this should extend across the whole leadership ecosystem of your organization.

In the next chapter, I explore what it means to take personal ownership for BRAVE leadership. We need systems for inclusive leadership to be sustainable, without a shadow of a doubt, but how do you become more BRAVE in your world? How do you lead by example, whether from the back, the centre or the front?

Chapter 6

Leading by example

The BRAVE leader is unapologetic about centring inclusion. They aim to be as thoughtful as possible when making sense of a situation, leveraging the best decision-making tools and then taking appropriate action.

If you expect those you lead to follow this lead, they need to have a sense of where you are going and what your expectations are. So you should be able to model this.

In this chapter, I double down on the practices that help you to lead by example.

Self-leadership is the practice of understanding who you are, identifying your desired experiences and intentionally guiding yourself towards them. It spans 'what' we do, 'why' we do it and 'how' we do it.

One of my clients demanded quite a lot from her staff. She often got frustrated by what she perceived as their lack of understanding of what she expected from them. Sometimes her direct reports would make decisions based on impulse rather than clear decision-making models. They showed lack of ability to manage conflict effectively within their teams, and very often their working patterns led to high stress and burnout.

As part of my coaching process with this client, I decided to do a 360-degree review. The person in question also does a self-evaluation to see how well their perception of themselves aligns with the views of others.

My emphasis in this process was to get a good sense, through a series of one-to-one interviews, of her leadership – what worked well, what areas could do with some improvement and what was notable about her leadership.

Overall, the feedback was good. She was seen as a determined leader, driven and quite articulate about where she wanted herself and her teams to go. She was somewhat surprised with some of the other feedback that came out of those interviews, though. It was suggested that she made decisions on impulse rather than using decision-making models, that she avoided conflict and others felt awkward when challenging her, and that her demands for information and drive to meet deadlines meant that she often seemed highly stressed, and that was passed on to the team.

So the problems she was highlighting in her team were the same issues that her team and some peers believed she needed to address herself. She should have been able to model the way for others to follow, but that was not happening.

We worked through these areas in the coaching sessions that followed. When I asked permission to include this case study, she was glad to give it. She was BRAVE enough to share this story, because she recognized that it could act as a useful example for others. She hoped that other leaders could become more self-aware and be able to lead by example.

If you expect a level of BRAVE leadership in your organization, one of the key ways to embed that is to demonstrate it yourself. As the Chinese philosopher Laozi said: 'Mastering others is strength. Mastering yourself is true power.'

Next, I explore how self-leadership can be developed to ensure inclusive leadership in your organization.

Managing your own performance

In Chapter 5, I spoke about performance management – how you can use it as an opportunity to help those you lead improve their performance by considering some questions.

As is the case for all staff in an organization, many leaders and high performers usually have their own performance outcomes set by those more senior in the organization. Whether through annual reviews, monthly check-ins, career development conversations or accountability meetings, performance management is usually shaped by someone else wanting to get the best value out of them, and this is very often tied to salary. This is done while staying in alignment with organizational goals of course.

In and of itself, there is nothing wrong with an organization wanting to measure performance, but what would happen if you were in control of your *own* performance? If you were given the opportunity to manage your own performance as a leader, what would be the key things that you would focus your energy on?

What are the things you would want to improve? What are the things you would want to remove from your scope of leadership? How would you want others you report to – be it your line manager, a board member or chair – to help you maximize your performance?

Let's look at how you can shape your own performance goals, rather than leaving it all up to others.

When I work with leaders on managing their own performance, one of the most challenging areas is motivation to commit to the parts of their work they least enjoy. You may be a senior manager or executive that hates working with numbers, but part of your job is to report back on your team's progress using statistics. You might hate doing one-to-ones or hosting meetings, but at the same time you are very aware that this is an important part of your role. So how do you get around doing those tasks you see as mundane or burdensome?

You might try to build these into your routine in a systematic way, rather than just leaving it to motivation or will power, which, let's face it, not many of us have when we are not enthralled about the task at hand. Systematizing your performance also allows you to keep track of what you do.

What can such a system look like? Well, it might include the following.

Goal setting

Set out the goals you want to achieve and how you are going to get there. Apply timelines for achieving your goals and schedule tasks to fit within this. As well as basic goals – the things that you *must* do as part of your job – the system should have goals that stretch your capabilities.

Time blocking

While for some leaders, simply working their way through to-do lists works really well, to get the most out of your time, you might consider time blocking. Here, you mark out times in your diary for specific tasks and meetings in any given week.

If you have a specific time blocked out, that introduces a level of accountability to do the specified tasks – you are not just waiting to feel motivated to do them. If you don't get through the set tasks, you know you will need to set out more time later on to get those done. This approach requires that you have control over your diary.

Accountability feedback

A system of feedback from people in your organization can also help to keep you on track. This is your personal advisory board, and it can include peers, line managers, sponsors, mentors and coaches. By checking in with those individuals at specific intervals on various issues, you become accountable for your progress, so you will rely less on having a whim to get things done.

No matter what things you need extra motivation to do, these tactics can be helpful. Note down the tasks, and ask those who are working with you and supporting you in your role as leader to make sure you are doing them.

This self-management system is set up so that you don't have to rely on feeling motivated to get things done. After you have established a system that works, you can focus on learning to improve your personal performance management.

Learning matters

I often ask leaders what training and development they have locked in for the year ahead. This is not about what others have planned for them, but the training, coaching or on-the-job learning they may want to pursue to fill gaps in their knowledge and skills.

I ask the following questions:

- Do you have the appropriate skills and learning to lead as well as possible?
- Have you made space for this development work in your schedule?
- What can those you lead learn from your own learning and development journey?
- What are the areas of leadership you feel less comfortable with and could do with more learning on?

- Is your learning Bold enough for others to want to do the same?

You never know enough. Even if you update your domain expertise in a constantly changing world, you can also prioritize learning for self-development and improving your own performance.

I will say that it should be something that you go into with an open mind and heart rather than with reluctance. Spend some time getting to understand the learning and development mission of your organization so that you can align your own personal development with that.

I have seen leaders resist training that they don't believe is relevant to the way they work. I've seen people recoil from what they consider mandatory learning or training – from conflict management to compliance to finance for non-finance leaders to unconscious bias training.

Very often when I go into organizations to speak on BRAVE leadership and why inclusion is important, I am at great pains to explain the importance of understanding it within the wider picture. The word 'inclusion' has put some people off, so I have to show how the process will add benefit for them and the organization.

The key is to look at your learning as something that will benefit not just you but the organization you work for as well, whether it is improving your communication skills, using new technology or understanding how to help shape your team or organization culture.

No matter how busy you are, there is always time to learn something new. If you mentor or support others, this is an ideal opportunity to show those aspiring leaders how you navigate learning for self-development, how you prioritize it even if your schedule is hectic.

Setting expectations

How often do you set expectations about yourself? Do people know your preferred ways of working? What boundaries do you set around times people can contact you?

It is very easy to be in your own head and think that you have explained to the people you lead how you like to work and what you expect from them, when in fact they are confused about what you want from them, when and how.

Also, I have been very mindful as I write this book that I am primarily doing so through the lens of European leadership styles. Part of my own learning journey is to learn more and more from leadership thinking outside this context.

While my setting of expectations sits within this particular perspective on leadership, you will want to explore what expectations look like within your own cultural context.

I am going to prompt you with a list of questions on ways of working so that you can think about your own preferences. These are questions I want you to consider when setting expectations of those impacted by your work.

- Do you know your preferred way of working? Is your dominant method to collaborate or work on issues on your own?
- What do you have in place to ensure that you don't get burnt out or tired?
- How do you share your personal values and what is important to you?
- What is your style for handing conflict?
- How do you prioritize your work?
- What are your preferred communication channels? Phone? Text? Instant message? Email? Group chat?

By identifying how you work best, you can send a clear message to those impacted by your work. This reduces so much stress in getting them to understand the way you see the world and how you operate.

If you are clearly able to articulate your preferred ways of working, you set expectations. But you also need to be able to adapt where those you lead do not share your style.

Let's say you are the kind of person who likes to deal with conflict head on. Then and there. You don't want an issue to be dragged out without resolution. It might be difficult for you to understand why someone else may need some time to process conflict.

Here, you can set the tone as a leader by telling the other person your expectations and explaining why it's important to move on, while also giving them a certain amount of time to respond and being flexible and inclusive enough to know when you must compromise in order to accommodate them.

This leans right back into the BRAVE model. You demonstrate Boldness by being clear about your expectations and inviting others to understand them, and you also hear from them what their expectations are. Resilience then becomes a team, rather than just an individual, thing. This is not just about how you respond to change but how your team can do the same. You demonstrate Agility when you show your way of working is not the dominant or only way of communicating. By leading the way and getting others to understand your way of working, you demonstrate being Visionary. And of course how you make decisions based on your way of working relates to being Ethical in leadership.

Modelling excellence

When I was growing up, 'discipline' was seen as a dirty word. It meant that if you didn't follow someone else's rules or regulations, you would be punished. Whether discipline came from my parents, my school teachers, my sports team or my church, it was always seen through the lens of compliance. If I didn't comply, then I was punished.

Of course the word has a different meaning as well, derived from the Latin word *discere*, which means 'to learn'. As I explored different schools of philosophy and thought, it further dawned on me that discipline in its true sense was about how we internalize learning and training.

Discipline is linked to how we make decisions. The whole point of this book is how you can leverage the tools and models available to you to have less fear and more courage and, in turn, make better decisions. This decision-making is not forced on you by external situations or individuals, but based on your own processing of information and contexts. It is how we learn, not just from the wins based on our decisions but also the mistakes we have made too.

When we see athletes, explorers, entrepreneurs and a host of others doing pioneering activities and thinking in different ways, we often frame that as self-discipline. Our world wants us to aspire to be like these influential figures and model excellence. Much of this goes hand in hand with having systems to keep us accountable, as discussed earlier. We can create habits and practise behaviours to bring discipline into the way we work.

I would like to suggest here that, as a BRAVE leader, you can model excellence, and next I describe three ways to approach this.

Consistency

Having spoken to thousands of people at live events, online and in my workshops and coaching groups, a recurring theme on what great leadership looks like is the focus on consistency.

Being BRAVE requires consistency. It is not about rebellion or being some kind of provocateur whenever decisions must be made. Rather, it is understanding what our value systems are, the behaviours that demonstrate those values and ultimately the rituals we have in place to ensure that we maintain those principles. At the heart of those rituals is consistency.

One of the most powerful statements I ever heard about values is that at some point they will cause you discomfort. Standing by what you care about can cause conflict if those values are ever breached. And when I talk about values here, I mean personal ones, not corporate ones. The ones you hold dear to your heart. It is your consistency around your values and the way you work that will make people understand what you stand for and get them to model your leadership.

There will be undoubtedly be times when you must make decisions in service of your team or organization that do not fit well with your personal values. It is being acutely aware of these that makes a difference. Consider the following questions:

- How are you being consistent in the way you lead?
- What has happened when you have not been consistent?
- Would you be Bold enough to ask questions of those who you lead about those times you have not been consistent?
- Would you be willing to take action on that feedback?

Your leadership will be assessed according to the consistency you demonstrate, not only in your decision-making but also in how you demonstrate self-leadership.

Active listening

'The world has way too many motivational speakers and not enough motivational leaders.'

I have used this line when I delivering keynotes around the globe on BRAVE leadership. Often I am met with bemused looks from people wondering what I am talking about. To get straight to the point, more people know how to talk than to listen. But as I say, I get to speak better and advise better based on the information I *listen* to first.

∼

One of my clients is a global bank that was struggling to understand why some of its brightest female talent in regional offices outside of Europe either never put themselves forward for leadership roles or weren't put forward by those who lead them.

I had a bag of tools that I knew I could deploy to help those women to leverage their personal and leadership brands, to have that executive voice and speak with authority, to tap into sponsorship and mentoring opportunities. But I quickly realized that the answer to this challenge was about actively listening to these women to try to understand what they thought the problem was.

What we uncovered from these sessions was a perception of leadership deeply at odds with the one I, living and working in London, was used to. This was a quieter, more collaborative model which respected hierarchy more than I was used to and needed a very different approach to address this leadership gap.

∼

This is the thing about active listening – it means you go into conversations without assumptions. You spend time parking your own biases so you can listen without interrupting. You repeat back what you heard for clarity and to understand what was being said. You focus on the person and what they are saying.

It is active in that through gestures and confirmations you demonstrate that you are present. That you read the room.

Even for those of us who practise active listening through coaching or consulting, there are still times when we need to sense-check. We must resist the temptation to jump in and finish with our own views.

It takes a BRAVE leader to do that, to actively listen even when under time constraints, when you have pressure from other stakeholders to get stuff done. It takes practice but you can get better with time. And when you can do it well and make those speaking feel listened to, it is worth it.

Impulse control

That reflection on active listening brings me to the third aspect of modelling excellence that I believe is important.

Have you ever been in a situation where someone got under your skin? Maybe they said something or sent an email or message that made you want to respond immediately with the wrath of God and all his angels?

What about taking action on a problem without carefully evaluating it? Or buying something based on an emotional rather than logical choice?

These are all examples of acting on impulse. Being impulsive might seem like you are being decisive in the moment, but it's important to think of the negative side of this.

If you are to make better and more BRAVE decisions, you must be emotionally aware and have thought things through, not only for yourself but for others who are looking to you for guidance through your leadership.

If you are impulsive, people are going to be forced to make decisions that match your impulsivity.

People will not want to be open, and they will hide mistakes they make.

People will model your behaviour because they think this is the way decisions are made, at least within your team or organization.

If you feel you are impulsive, try asking those around you who you are accountable to.

Taking care of yourself

Establish clear boundaries between work and personal life. Demonstrate the importance of taking time off, unplugging from work and engaging in activities that promote relaxation and rejuvenation. By respecting your own boundaries and not being on call – after all, you're not a surgeon saving lives (unless of course you are!) – you show your reports and team members that it is essential to prioritize personal wellbeing.

Leaders should take regular breaks during the work day to recharge and avoid burnout. I see so much resistance to this. So many people needlessly tell themselves that if they go on a break, the world will go to hell in a handbasket. If you are empowering people to make decisions in your presence, then give them agency to make the same decisions in your absence. Use vacation time to rest, recharge and spend time with family and friends. By taking breaks and vacations, leaders demonstrate the importance of rest and rejuvenation.

Prioritize your physical and mental health by engaging in activities that promote wellbeing. This can include regular exercise, eating nutritious meals, getting enough sleep and practising stress management techniques. By prioritizing health and wellness, you demonstrate to direct reports and other team members the importance of taking care of yourself.

Do not hesitate to seek support when needed. This can include reaching out to mentors, coaches or therapists for guidance and advice. By demonstrating a willingness to seek support, leaders promote the importance of mental and emotional wellbeing.

It may seem strange to some when practitioners like myself speak or coach (and now write) about this, but getting leaders to engage in regular self-reflection and mindfulness practices is dope. This can involve journaling, meditation or other techniques that help them stay present and connected with their own thoughts and emotions. By practising self-reflection and mindfulness, leaders model the importance of self-awareness and emotional balance.

I am not the biggest fan of the term 'work–life balance'. I prefer to talk about a 'blend'. Sometimes you have to work long hours or to high-pressure deadlines. Other times, not so much. Essentially, this is not about avoiding excessive work hours, but knowing this doesn't have to be the norm for all work. Learn to delegate tasks, and make time for personal interests and relationships. Get a life. There is more than just work. (I know some readers will hate me for that line, but I am going to be *brave* and stick with it.) By demonstrating the work–life blend, you show that success does not have to come at the expense of personal wellbeing.

You can actively promote self-care practices within your team. This can involve discussing the importance of self-care, providing resources or information on wellness topics and encouraging team members to prioritize their own wellbeing. By fostering a culture of self-care, leaders create an environment that supports and values the wellbeing of their team members.

In addition, in the modern era, people are not as afraid as they used to be to focus on people's different learning styles, and this subsequently prioritizes mental as well as physical wellbeing.

I cannot emphasize enough the need to allocate dedicated time for personal development and growth. This can involve reading, attending workshops or seminars and engaging in activities, like storytelling and scenario planning, that enhance leadership skills. By investing in your own development, you demonstrate the importance of continuous learning and growth.

Embracing failure

Own up when you screw up.

The message is simple: don't be afraid to own it when you do things wrong. It is way too easy to give the impression you are perfect when, as we all know, no one is.

A caveat: If you are in culture that does not deal with owning mistakes, then of course it is very possible that you will be reluctant to take this course of action. As I mentioned before when talking about impulse control, if you are working in a climate of fear, there will be a reluctance to own up. Sometimes being BRAVE around owning mistakes can threaten a leader's job security. But also, if you value things like honesty and integrity, being able to own your mistakes will be important to you.

But for now, let's assume that you have the opportunity own your mistakes. Here are some options to help you lean into admitting your mistake.

If you have made a mistake and you know that it has an effect on others who are impacted by your work, then it is OK to admit and apologize. Saying sorry when you mess up doesn't make you any less of a leader. In fact, I would argue it makes you more of a BRAVE leader than those who choose to hold back from doing this.

When you own your mistake, you are modelling to others that they too can take responsibility when they mess up. It is possible that the reason many leaders don't take this approach is fear about what others may think. They might wonder: Do people see me as incompetent? Will they trust my leadership? Is being BRAVE about this going to stop me from being embarrassed?

There is a chance you will be embarrassed or even frustrated with yourself when you make a mistake. That is a normal human emotion. We are social animals and no matter how tough we may appear on the outside, inevitably we will feel a little something.

Once you have owned the mistake, there is an opportunity to look at why that mistake was made.

A client of mine is the chief financial officer (CFO) of a tech company. In his reporting function, he realized a financial scenario that he and one of his direct reports had been working on had an error that overstated how robust the company would be in the face of certain external impacts. In this case, it was a sudden change in interest rates.

In one of our sessions, I realized he looked really uncomfortable and I asked if he was willing to share what was really on his mind. He hesitated and said he would like to but it was an accounting matter and he wasn't sure I would understand. I reminded him I was an accountant in one of my former careers and asked him to give it a shot.

After explaining his model and assumptions, we walked through how he could not only own this error but also correct it. The quick, steady rise in interest rates could partially explain the issue, but it would be better to be open about the assumptions made and explain to the organization that he and his team had since built an even more robust model. The formulas and guardrails in place would be able to detect anomalies or discrepancies much earlier that was the case with the earlier model.

He was terrified to go to the board and explain, as he felt they would see him as incompetent. We walked through all the times he had actually improved financial efficiency and awareness in the company, and we also looked at how he could explain that while an error had been made, it was caught soon enough to avoid too much damage in relation to the organization's reporting to stakeholders.

With this CFO, I got him to clearly define what the mistake was, think of a way he could communicate the error to his various stakeholders and reports, define a plan of action in order to recover from the mistake, put guardrails in policies and processes to prevent a mistake like this from happening again and then track that process.

In sum, when you make a mistake, you should:

- Own the mistake.
- Own your reactions to that mistake.
- Understand why the mistake was made.
- Communicate clearly to those affected that a mistake was made.
- Determine and clarify how the mistake will be fixed.
- Use it, where appropriate, as a learning tool.

Showing self-leadership around how you manage mistakes is also a great way of coaching others how to handle conflict and mistakes.

Asking better questions

My final recommendation about self-leadership involves questioning.

It is a BRAVE thing for a leader to try to ask better questions.

Often the big mistakes that can be made by leaders are because they have made assumptions rather than asking questions.

Take this question: How can we work better together between performance reviews?

I love this question. I have had leaders say to me: 'Why should I ask this question? Am I not paying them to come up with the answer?'

There is something about getting into the habit of asking good questions. In fact, asking questions that inspire a sense of creativity as well as deeper and more critical thinking, I believe, can empower those who you lead to be on their top game.

My wife used to work in sales and she explained to me the difference between open and closed questions. I hated selling but learned to love it more when I really grasped the concept of these kinds of questions.

For the record, an open question is one that cannot be answered with a simple 'yes' or 'no' response. It is phrased so as to elicit a longer response.

Closed questions, on the other hand, are phrased so as to elicit a 'yes' or 'no' response.

Let's go back to the question above about performance reviews to see how this looks as an open question and a closed question.

How can we work better together? This is an open question because it requires the person answering to really think about how you can collaborate.

Do you need my help? This is a closed question. It doesn't require more than a 'yes' or 'no' answer and doesn't necessarily lead to expansive thinking, especially if the person responding is waiting for you to ask all the questions.

So much of my coaching is shaped around asking my clients questions. Not to trip them up or bamboozle them with my wisdom of models, but rather to get them to think through their answers and how they can apply ideas to their lives and ways of working. A great question helps the person discover something about themselves they've never realized before.

Two books which have hugely shaped the way I ask questions are *Leading with Questions* by Michael Marquardt and Bob Tiede and *Power Questions* by Andrew Sobel and Jerold Panas.[10]

Both of these books have helped not only me but those I have coached to think about how we ask questions of ourselves and of others.

They have helped me to be more BRAVE when I ask questions.

I have become more aware of the kind of questions I am asking, and I consider how inclusive I am when asking them.

---

[10] M. Marquardt and B. Tiede, *Leading with Questions: How Leaders Discover Powerful Answers by Knowing How and What to Ask*, 3rd edition (2023); A. Sobel and J. Panas, *Power Questions: Build Relationships, Win New Business, and Influence Others* (2012).

I test which questions land well and what kind of responses I get when I ask them to different groups of people.

I am more aware of what I am trying to accomplish with the questions I am asking, and I interrogate my own attachment to words and meanings as well as the assumptions that I may hold which inform my questions.

I often ask permission of my clients to go deeper with questions. I do so consciously because it is very easy to be blasé and ignore their past experiences. Asking for permission allows the conversation to be a collaboration rather than an inquisition. I also use this as a teaching moment to get my clients to think about questions they would ask of themselves as well as what they would ask of others.

Let me give some examples of the kind of questions you can ask yourself, let's say at the end of a working day:

- What really worked for me today as a leader?
- What didn't work or frustrated the heck out of me?
- What things can I improve on?
- How did I demonstrate leadership today?
- How was I BRAVE today?
- What did I learn today that I can implement tomorrow?
- What did I do to keep myself accountable today?
- Who did I call on to check my accountability?

I am sure you can add to this, but asking questions like these is how you start to become more aware of how you show up as a leader. You can use this kind of questioning as a testing ground for how you can ask better questions of others.

Asking better questions helps you to be more courageous and make better decisions. The starting point is exploring what you do well and what you can do to improve, and asking yourself about the impact you have on others.

I would like to finish off this section by also saying that context is everything. There will be some times when you need to hold back from asking questions, but the key point here is that when you do ask questions of yourself and of others, you should demonstrate what good questions look like.

BRAVE leadership starts with yourself.

Getting to grips with self-leadership is not an easy task. Like any muscle, it needs training and exercise and focus.

Now I have examined the practices and benefits of leadership, I will talk about how coaching will give you and your leaders an advantage.

Chapter 7

The coaching advantage

What is leadership coaching?

Even though this may seem like stating the obvious, I think it is important for people to understand what leadership coaching is. It is not therapy. It is not consulting.

Leadership coaching is a process where a professional coach works closely with an individual, team or group to enhance their leadership abilities, skills and effectiveness. It is a collaborative partnership between the coach and the client, with the aim of helping the client to develop leadership potential, overcome obstacles and achieve goals.

It focuses on improving leadership competencies, such as self-awareness, which I focused on in the last chapter. It also explores communication, decision-making, problem-solving, strategic thinking and emotional intelligence.

The coach provides guidance, support and feedback to the client, helping them identify their strengths and areas for development. The coaching process typically involves a series of one-on-one coaching sessions where the coach and the client engage in open, and confidential, conversations where the coach uses various techniques, questioning strategies and assessments to facilitate self-reflection, learning and growth. They may also provide relevant resources, tools and exercises to assist the client in their leadership development journey.

It is not about providing direct solutions or advice, but rather empowering the client to discover their own insights, make informed choices and take purposeful actions. It helps leaders like you gain clarity, build confidence, improve leadership skills and achieve professional and organizational objectives.

In my leadership coaching, some common threads appear across the clients I work with, but the context will always be specific to the client. I fully appreciate that the leadership challenges faced by boards, executive teams, country managers and team leaders are so different and context specific, so I make sure that whatever tools and strategies I employ to help my clients tackle challenges, we agree on desired outcomes, boundaries and how we will measure the impact of the coaching.

How does coaching help with inclusive leadership?

Leadership coaching, especially how I do it, using the BRAVE model, is specifically designed to get clients thinking about inclusion. It is intentionally focused on being considerate of the reach and impact of the decisions made by leaders like you. It helps to inform how you make sense of the world and ultimately the action you take.

Such coaching tends to be delivered differently depending on the target audience I am working with, specifically whether that is executives, groups or teams.

Executive coaching

In this book, I have included a few case studies from my work as an executive coach. I use coaching because I believe it is more effective than training for what I am trying to achieve.

This doesn't take away from training as a method of leadership development. On the contrary, it is complementary to this form of development. However, coaching is more tailored and speaks to specific issues that the client is facing.

Most of my leadership coaching is targeted at senior to mid-level executives working in high-performance cultures. The areas I tend to focus my coaching on include:

- performance improvement;
- leadership progression;
- succession planning;
- executive presence and influence;
- stakeholder management;
- presentations skills; and
- leading boards and executive committees.

One of the reasons my coaching works well is that I provide an insight into how things look from an outside view. No emotional attachment, no company cultural bubble, just a straightforward perspective on how things look from the outside.

Executive coaching can help the client to explore aspects associated with individual performance, such as self-awareness, decision-making processes, opportunities and scenario planning. It can also make you aware of things that may hold you back – blind spots, negative thinking and even dealing with feelings of inferiority or being out of place.

It also looks at technical and commercial aspects around executive leadership – for example, focusing on strategy, stakeholder management, financial planning, the talent journey and operations management.

Working on this combination of the personal and the commercial is part of my USP. Knowing the commercial side and pressures placed on my clients as well as the internal dialogue that they have to unpack is crucial to the success of my work.

Take this scenario: a client is staying up late trying to balance the profit and loss of a business unit before meeting with the senior management team the next day. It is one thing to understand this from a technical point of view and a whole other thing to appreciate and empathize with the kind of emotions that will influence decision-making when under this sort of pressure. Training can be done around the principles of navigating finance or even to improve emotional intelligence, but with coaching the context moves beyond scenarios to actual, real-world issues. So the conversations are not just about theory but what is happening in that moment.

Group coaching

Group coaching is aimed at a group within an organization. Group members may work in a specific function – finance, marketing, customer service and so on. Or they may have a certain level of seniority – country managers, division heads, line managers and so on. The point is they are all in a session to address a collective challenge or theme around their leadership.

Let me walk you through what I mean by this.

~

One of my clients is a digital marketing company. Many leaders in the organization believed the culture was one of belonging and equity. After all, that's what it said on the website. Following a series of in-house surveys, they realized that while the intentions of leaders were well meant, the true experience of many employees showed that the culture was far from welcoming. The data came back to say that female and non-white members of staff were less likely to progress in their roles and more likely to leave.

For some of the leaders, this wasn't something they ever had to address before, and there was some resistance as to why the protected characteristics of sex and race were used as identifiers for staff.

My group coaching session was designed to explore the data, address some of the key points raised and then use a strengths-based approach (appreciative inquiry, which I talk about later) to see how this group could improve the situation. As with many group settings like this, my job as a facilitator was to make sure that no matter how challenging the conversation was, people would feel safe enough to ask tough questions but also be able to sit in discomfort. We could have BRAVE conversations and be OK with the reality that there would be no easy answers for some of the questions raised.

Group coaching for leaders is a great way to energize and motivate members of that group to work towards a common goal. Whether this is facilitated by external coaches like myself or run by someone within the organization, it lends itself well to the BRAVE model of coaching. For instance:

- Can members of the group be Bold enough to speak their truth?
- Can they be just as Bold to sit with realities different from what they thought was true?
- What can be learned from these sessions that can bond the members and improve Resilience?
- What ways can questions be asked to shape how Ethical leadership is viewed in the group?

Whether a group is facing some kind of crisis or looking to improve the way they can grow their organization, the purpose of group coaching will be to empower clients to take a leap towards making better decisions.

Team coaching

Team coaching is slightly different. Although it may seem similar to group coaching, the focus here is a lot more around connection and specific team goals.

This kind of coaching tends to focus more on executive committees, boards or senior leadership teams. But it can be around any team with a specific goal in mind that they wish to achieve.

One of my clients ran a fast-growing energy company. When I first started working with them, they were on the cusp of being acquired by a larger UK holding company. Any acquisition by a larger company brings several great opportunities to scale up and reach bigger financial and customer acquisition targets, but it also brings some challenges around culture. Ways of working in two different companies don't suddenly become aligned just because they share an investor, directors or company branding.

In addition to how they would navigate culture change, there was an expectation placed on my client that they would be able to scale up their operations. This meant that the executive team had to learn not only how to make decisions alone but also how to do this together, often at speed and, most importantly, being aware of how they communicated that to each other.

Front of mind is how decisions are made inclusively. This doesn't mean that everything needs to be done by a committee or that there needs to be a 'tick box' approach to try and cover every eventuality. Rather, the focus for me as a coach is to remind the collective executive team about the fundamental needs and requirements to be considered when they are making decisions, problem-solving or taking action.

This work is usually done with a lot of stakeholders in mind, and it often involves things like 360-degree reviews or staff interviews to get a full view of how the members of the team are perceived around the organization.

Internal coaching

The two kinds of coaching I've discussed so far tend to be seen by many as the domain of external coaches. And yet there is a huge advantage in organizations developing a culture of internal coaching.

While an external coach can come and intervene with leaders across the board, some of the tools and techniques used by external coaches can be deployed internally as well. For instance, coaching techniques can be used internally to:

- better manage conflict;
- discover blind spots in leadership; and
- encourage more inclusive decision-making.

~

One of my clients was a global bank that wanted to address a gap in leadership opportunities for Black and Black mixed heritage staff. They noticed that in feedback from across a number of business areas, many of these staff didn't believe they had opportunities for career and leadership progression, and some thought the bank was deliberately working towards preventing such progression.

I suggested a sponsorship programme to help address this gap. I would coach the aspirational members of staff as to how they could ask better questions of their sponsors so as to navigate this terrain. I would also work with sponsors and coach them on how best to have BRAVE and sometimes difficult conversations with a cohort who had a mixed bag of experiences they weren't aware of.

I coached sponsors on how they could help sponsees to navigate imposter syndrome or communicate more effectively, without the burden of being seen as aggressive instead of assertive. I coached sponsees on how they could communicate upwards and got them to think about why they were reluctant to ask for new roles. I also coached them on how to explain that they avoided conflict as they didn't want to jeopardize their roles as the primary income earner in their households or wider families.

The idea was to equip both the sponsors and sponsees with coaching toolkits that would help them navigate their own challenges, but also allow them to coach up and, as they progressed in their own careers, to coach direct reports and others who came behind them.

I recommend a lovely little book called *The Coaching Habit*[11] to all my coaching clients. Given that most of them are senior executives and managers, or at least aspiring to be, this is my way of getting them to think a bit more like a coach, primarily around asking better questions but also how they can listen better and think more strategically. I smile a bit when I think I can hand this book to them.

Coaching using the BRAVE model

There are three core coaching models that have shaped my inclusive leadership coaching: systemic coaching, appreciative inquiry and polarity thinking. These are my preferred coaching models as they fit with the principles of the BRAVE model, as I will explain through this section.

I do realize if you have no intention of being a coach, then learning or adopting those models for inclusive leadership may not be something you would aim to do. That said, I believe it is important to explain why coaching is a core part of the approach to embedding inclusive or BRAVE leadership into your organization.

Systemic coaching

The premise of Peter Hawkins and Eve Turner's *Systemic Coaching*[12] is that coaching needs to step up to deliver value

---

[11] M.B. Stainer, *The Coaching Habit: Say Less, Ask More and Change the Way You Lead Forever* (2016).

[12] P. Hawkins and E. Turner, *Systemic Coaching: Delivering Value Beyond the Individual* (2019).

to all those who are affected by the work of the person being coached. This would include those they lead, colleagues, investors, customers, partners, their local community and also the wider organizational ecology.

Systemic coaching simply deploys a point of view that acknowledges relationships and system dynamics beyond the individual. Teams, a group of people who share a common purpose, are themselves systems, as well as being part of a wider system – for example, within the organization, within an industry and within a cultural or regulatory context.

In my work, I get clients to map the systems they work in, which are known as constellations. I use this approach to move just beyond the individual and look at the system. What is the culture and climate of the organization they work in? What are the values, beliefs and policies in that organization and, ultimately, how are these perceived by clients and other stakeholders?

This helps to provide a framework for improving workplace dynamics, increasing psychological safety and improving employee retention, among other things. By getting the people I coach to see their development within the context of a system, rather than just relating to them as individuals, they can explore behavioural outcomes instead of just the personal challenges the individuals may have.

One of the reasons I lean heavily on systemic coaching is that it really resonates with the key elements of the BRAVE model. Systemic leadership coaching asks us to be Bold in getting our clients to see leadership as something that should be embedded in the organization rather than our individual client's skills. It asks us to be Resilient by adapting to the needs of our clients or the challenges of supervision and Agile enough to draw on new models and ways of thinking to help our clients. It asks us to be Visionary in our ambitions for the outcomes of our coaching and Ethical by respecting both individual and organizational needs for a healthy coaching relationship. It turns on its head the myth that leadership is about singular acts by charismatic individuals and gets us to examine the core beliefs and behaviours that inform and shape the leadership DNA of organizations.

Appreciative inquiry

The second coaching model I describe here is appreciative inquiry.[13]

This is a strengths-based approach to coaching, where the focus is not on weaknesses but the assets your leadership and organization has.

Appreciative enquiry allows for examination of best practices and helps in developing strategic plans and shifting culture for individual leaders, teams and groups. While systemic coaching definitely explores the good and the bad of the system, appreciative inquiry focuses more on the strengths that exist both within and without the organization.

This is aimed squarely at how to get leaders, at team and organizational levels, to reinforce the things that work. This might be to do with relationships, practices and processes that help to foster collaboration, innovation, accountability or other elements that help to push the organization forward.

This coaching model is delivered through four stages: discovery, dream, design and destiny.

Discovery

My clients explore 'the best of what is', identifying their team's or their organization's strengths, best practices and sources of excellence, vitality and peak performance.

---

13 D.L. Cooperrider and D. Whitney, *Appreciative Inquiry: A Positive Revolution in Change* (2005).

Dream

They envision a future they really want – a future where the organization is fully engaged and successful around its core purpose and strategic objectives.

Design

They leverage the best of 'what is' and their visions for the future to design high-impact strategies that move the organization creatively and decisively in the right direction.

Destiny

They put the strategies into action, revising as necessary.

This tool allows me as a coach to focus on my clients' strengths.

If you are going to be Bold, you need to know your strengths. The same with Resilience. I think you get the drift.

Let me give some examples of questions I may use as part of this process when coaching teams.

- What do you value the most about how you work as a team?
- What do you see as the three most desirable things about your team, which you can build on for success?
- What specific strengths were you and your teammates showing during the project?
- What stories did you tell each other in order to achieve your goals?

Although the emphasis here is on strengths and what works, the possibility that there may be frailties or weakness within the team is not ignored. The objective of this inquiry is to explore the team or organization through an asset-based lens and then, where there may be challenges, to raise them in consideration of the strengths that already exist.

Polarity thinking

This leads me to polarity thinking,[14] my third default coaching tool.

A fellow coach brought this model to my attention a few years ago, and it has come to be one of the most powerful tools in my coaching toolkit.

For many leaders, situations are seen through the lens of 'either/or' – in other words, binary thinking.

Polarity thinking, on the other hand, sees truth and wisdom on more than one side of an issue, and each side is incomplete without the wisdom and input of the other.

Very often, seeing things in either/or terms can limit leaders' sense-making and strength of decision-making. But using polarity thinking and not being afraid of being wrong or exploring beyond binary options can help leaders decide what approach they can use to solve an issue.

As Abraham Maslow said: 'If the only tool you have is a hammer, it is tempting to treat everything as if it were a nail.'[15] What polarity thinking allows people who are being coached to do is see beyond a single solution for a problem.

As I write this book, leaders are facing a multitude of challenges in the workplace. Remote working. Challenging economic times. The threat of AI to existing roles and ways of working. The constant political challenges to culture.

Polarity thinking gives a moment to pause for thought before making impulsive and rash binary decisions. It is a joy to see clients who will use Polarity Maps[16] – a matrix tool used for polarity thinking – to explore how they will strategically plan ahead or tackle problems in the present.

---

[14] See the Polarity Partnerships website at: www.polaritypartnerships.com

[15] A.H. Maslow, *The Psychology of Science: A Reconnaissance* (1966).

[16] See the Polarity Partnerships website at: www.polaritypartnerships.com

Tying these back to the BRAVE model

It is all well and good having these tools, but what is of paramount importance to me is how I can use them in the BRAVE model to help my clients around sense-making and making good decisions.

- How can these tools encourage Bold decision-making?
- In what ways can these tools reinforce Resilience?
- In what ways can polarity thinking help us to lead with Agility?
- Where can we show examples of an inclusive Visionary leadership using these tools?
- How can we demonstrate Ethical leadership?

What excites me about sharing these principles in this book is that you get to think more about how you can apply them to your ways of working. How you can shape the BRAVE model to the cultural context of your organization, or the division and region of your department in a global organization?

Theory of change

I am working on building a theory of change for the BRAVE model of coaching as I continue to develop it with my team.

I am following the six steps as laid out by the folks at the Center for the Theory of Change.

1. Identify long-term goals.
2. Backwards map and connect the preconditions and requirements necessary to achieve the goals. Explain why these preconditions are necessary and sufficient.
3. Identify your basic assumptions about the context.
4. Identify the interventions that will create your desired change.

5. Develop indicators to measure outcomes.
6. Write a narrative to explain the logic of the interventions.[17]

The last two steps are important. I want all of this coaching and the different approaches to making inclusion more acceptable as a function of leadership to be tried, tested and replicable. Across cultures where possible. Learning and iterating as we go along to make it as good as we can.

I do not want to base this approach just on anecdotal evidence. I want to draw on data from my work and the work of my team to test this thinking. To see how BRAVE plays out for real for leaders across different organizations.

It is also important to understand what the BRAVE model means for leaders and systems that have different ways of working based on regional nuances and particular cultural expectations.

I believe the BRAVE model can impact ways of working in London or Lagos, Buenos Aires or Beijing, Massachusetts or Munich. It especially helps me when working with global clients. The principles can be adapted whether we are coaching locally or globally.

At present, my theory of change for BRAVE looks like this:

1. My long-term goals are to test and try the BRAVE model as a viable leadership model and move it beyond a narrative of just talent management.
2. I am mapping backwards to understand and connect the preconditions and requirements necessary to achieve these goals. From writing content like this

---

[17] Adapted from Center for the Theory of Change, 'How does theory of change work?' Available from: www.theoryofchange. org/what-is-theory-of-change/how-does-theory-of-change-work/ [accessed 20 November 2023].

to speaking about it and testing theories as to how it works across different contexts.

3. I am learning why these preconditions are necessary and sufficient.

4. My basic assumptions about the context are that inclusive leadership, especially through the lens of the BRAVE model, is practice and sector agnostic. With the help of some sharper minds than mine, I am testing how coaching especially helps to drive my desired change.

5. I am working in partnership with others to develop specific indicators to measure outcomes.

6. At some point, I get to write a deeper narrative to explain the logic of the interventions.

My theory of change is a dynamic work in progress. The assumptions that I lean on in version one of this book may change in future editions, but we shall see.

Let's move on to how to build teams and manage resistance using inclusive leadership.

Chapter 8

Team building and managing resistance

So far, I have been extolling the virtues of inclusive leadership and the role it plays in developing yourself, your team and your organization in order to become more robust. But, let's be honest here, this is not by any measure going to be a walk in the park. Leadership development is never straightforward.

Change management is hard. Culture change is not easy, and I will delve into a bit of that in the next chapter for sure. But first I would really love to explore what being a BRAVE leader looks like around team building.

The purpose of inclusive team building is to foster a sense of belonging, collaboration and productivity within a diverse group of individuals. Inclusive team building aims to create an environment where every team member feels valued, respected and empowered to contribute their unique perspectives, skills and experiences.

Team building objectives

There are a number key objectives for inclusive team building. I would like to explore some of them before jumping into the 'how' of building inclusive teams.

The first is about building trust and respect. There is no way you can have an inclusive team unless team members feel valued and heard. I think there should be a clear boundary here – just because you have a strong opinion or even data, it doesn't mean that your view has to be prioritized. That said, the ethos should be that there is an environment of trust and respect which in turn enhances cooperation, reduces conflict and improves communication within the team.

Many organizations work with individuals from varied and diverse backgrounds. It is a BRAVE act to create a space for all team members to be able to be active contributors to your team without having to second-guess trust and respect.

Inclusive team building fosters collaboration by encouraging teamwork and cooperation. This is not about shiny away days or drinks after work, but rather an intentional bringing together of individuals with diverse skills and perspectives. In essence, this allows teams to tackle problems from multiple angles, leading to more effective problem-solving and creative solutions.

Leaders are encouraged to seek ways of improving that collaboration. This might involve asking better questions, listening to concerns and being OK with being challenged.

There are countless pieces of research demonstrating how collaboration boosts morale and motivation. When team members feel included, recognized and appreciated, this enhances their motivation and morale. So it seems almost self-evident that if you create a positive and supportive environment where individuals can thrive, that will result in increased job satisfaction and productivity. But apparently it doesn't happen enough – hence me asking you to be the BRAVE ones and challenge that norm.

So let's talk about effective communication.

I am sure you and others have heard ad infinitum about the value of effective communication and active listening. It encourages open dialogue, the exchange of ideas and the understanding of different viewpoints, which under your leadership can improve team dynamics, foster clearer communication channels and build stronger relationships among team members. I address resistance to this later in the chapter, but never underestimate the power of effective communication, and don't be afraid to build in systems that support it.

The final objective for building inclusive teams is to encourage the participation and engagement of different individuals. Including people from different backgrounds, cultures, genders, age groups and so on can add massive value to your organization and also aid your development as a leader. Diversity entails a wide range of talents, insights and ideas that can lead to innovation and better decision-making.

And this is what BRAVE leadership is all about. Better decision-making from the ground up.

Building inclusive teams

So now we are clear about the objectives for building inclusive teams, let's have a look at how it can be done.

Clarity

Clarity is essential for building effective teams.

Clear communication enables team members to align their efforts with their own values and those of the organization, understand expectations and work towards shared goals. It eliminates confusion, reduces errors and fosters trust and collaboration.

I am a big fan of teams making sure that they are clear about their ways of working.

Here is a template I use with a number of my clients – this follows a format that is used in an awesome online resource called Manual of Me, which is a free tool to help you communicate to people your preferred way of working.[18]

Hi my name is _____

---

[18] You can access this at: manualof.me

Here are some of the fundamental things you should know about me _____
My working hours are fixed/flexible and I prefer to be contacted _____
My ideal working environment is _____
And my preferred methods of communication are _____

I add value to those I work with by _____
The best way to give me feedback is _____

Clarity about how the team works together is just as important.

When leading a team, you should make sure everyone knows:

- what goals you are trying to achieve;
- why you are trying to achieve them;
- what strategies you will be using to achieve them;
- what role each member plays in the team; and
- what is expected from these roles.

You can add other points, but if there is clarity and purpose around what you are trying to achieve as a team, then it is so much easier to make decisions.

Team goals and objectives

As noted, it is a must to communicate your team's purpose, priorities and desired outcomes to ensure that everyone is on the same page.

Clear goals help team members understand the bigger picture and align their efforts accordingly. Goals should provide a clear direction and a framework for evaluating progress. Regularly revisit and communicate these goals to ensure ongoing clarity and focus.

If you don't know where you are going, how will you know when you have got there?

This may seem really obvious to some people, but I have lost count of the number of times I've worked with team members who have no idea what their goals and objectives actually are.

Managing expectations

Clear expectations allow team members to understand what is required of them and how their contributions lead to team success.

In Chapter 6, on leading by example, I spoke about setting out clear expectations about yourself. It is just as important to set expectations about your team. In some cultures, expectations about team working take priority over personal boundaries. Regardless of how you come to it, you cannot manage expectations unless you set them.

Leaders should articulate performance expectations, deliverables, deadlines and quality standards explicitly. It is your responsibility to provide clear guidelines on roles and responsibilities, including the division of tasks and decision-making authority. Additionally, BRAVE leaders will seek to explore how inclusive these can be.

I know this seems like a long list but stick with me.

It is important to establish communication protocols for how and when information should be shared within the team. To reinforce a shared understanding of expectations, check in regularly with team members and clarify any points that team members are not sure about and answer any questions. Establish regular team meetings, both formal and informal, to provide opportunities for dialogue and ensure that everyone stays informed. Transparent communication builds trust, reduces misunderstandings and strengthens team dynamics.

This doesn't mean meeting overload or filling messaging services with needless data and updates, but agreeing on the importance and regularity of interactions is key.

Encourage your team members to share information, insights and concerns openly. To prioritize, be transparent. I touch on this a little bit more when I speak about candour, but the main point is that establishing a practice of courageous and open contributions helps the overall success of the team.

You know your people and the culture of your organization, so create an environment where people feel comfortable expressing their thoughts, opinions and ideas. You should set the example by actively seeking and sharing information, maintaining transparency and encouraging questions and feedback (as I mentioned in Chapter 6).

Avoid jargon or the overuse of technical terms, or those crazy mnemonics that so many leaders are fond of. Also note that ambiguous phrases may lead to confusion. Always be clear.

Encourage team members to articulate their ideas in a straightforward manner, using simple language that is easily understood by all. And when you are providing instructions, feedback or explanations, be precise and specific. I know how leaders love an acronym (as I do, with the BRAVE model), especially in larger organizations. This in and of itself is not a problem as long as the message is clear. Mix it up a bit and consider using visual aids, such as diagrams or charts, to enhance clarity and comprehension, but don't let that become a crutch. A simple litmus test is could you still explain the point if the electricity went out and you couldn't start up your PowerPoint, Keynote, Prezi or whatever. Regularly check in with team members to make sure they understand your ideas. Ask them to summarize or restate important points to ensure that they've picked up on things correctly. You can never ever overstate enough if people don't get it first time around.

The last point here is on active listening. I mentioned this in Chapter 6 as a way to model leadership excellence.

We have two ears and mouth for a reason, and listening is a key component of clear communication within teams. Encourage team members to listen attentively to one another and seek to understand before responding.

Active listening demonstrates respect, fosters empathy and minimizes misinterpretation. Leaders should also provide regular feedback to team members, both individually and collectively, to enhance clarity. Feedback should be specific, timely and focused on behaviours and outcomes, providing guidance for improvement. Create a feedback culture that values continuous learning and growth, allowing team members to align their actions with expectations and make necessary adjustments.

Candour

Teams thrive when they are open and honest and frank. The notion of candour may seem strange to some but let me explain what I mean by this term.

If you are leading a team and you want to have clearly defined conversations with people, it is important that you are aware of the best forms of communication in your team. Some leaders push back, saying that they don't have the time do this. My response is: How can you lead inclusively if you don't take the time to understand the best forms of communication?

Inclusion doesn't mean that you are subject to people's whims and specific needs, but rather that you have an understanding of how people perceive and understand your messaging and, in turn, you learn how they wish to be perceived and understood.

There will always be a mix of personalities and experiences in teams. Although the overall purpose of the team is paramount, given the work you must do, there is something to be said about also tapping into different communication styles.

What works in terms of candour for a team in America may not necessarily work in a team in Angola, Brazil, China, Germany or India. It is especially important for leaders to be aware of this when communicating with teams that work across territories.

Cultural awareness

A term I came across when discussing courage and honesty with a US client is 'radical candour'.[19] It is defined as saying what you think while also being considerate of the person you're saying it to.

If you tried taking this to cultures where hierarchy, context and formality are given primacy, you will have had a great deal of problems.

In 2020, while working with a client, I was approached to give some workshop sessions on BRAVE conversations that could be had in a workplace around race and ethnicity and around class. One of the key offices where I was expected to deliver a session in was in India, but the leaders in that office pushed back against this.

The honest feedback I got from individuals was that if I did not fully understand hierarchy and the nuances of workplace power, I could end up causing more damage. My initial reaction to this was to question their motives (silently at least), wondering if they were afraid of being BRAVE. I came to realize, on reflection, that even if there was a global leadership directive being

---

[19] Kim Scott, *Radical Candour: How to Get What You Want by Saying What You Mean* (2017).

driven to tackle issues around race and ethnicity, my sessions wouldn't land unless I understood not just the workplace culture but the nuances of the wider societal culture.

I never did get to deliver this programme, but with subsequent global clients that wanted to resolve some tough issues in the workplace, I was able to take the time at first to discover more about the context. This involved me having discovery meetings to see what worked in the particular context and what kind of behaviour change would be sustainable.

Candour in these situations was still about honesty and courage, but this was wrapped up in an understanding of the local context of the clients. What works in one territory doesn't necessarily work in another.

In different cultural settings, communication styles may be closer to 'high-context communication' or 'low-context communication'.

High-context communication tends to exist in countries and groups where there is little racial diversity. Group needs or collectivism are more valued than individual needs, be they to do with work, family or the wider culture. People have a very strong sense of identity, steeped in history and tradition, with values intrinsically linked to this and with little sense of change. There is a clear demarcation between those considered insiders and outsiders.

Non-verbal cues, through tone, eye contact, gestures and facial expressions, have as much currency as the words that are spoken. Conflict is often tied to misinterpretation of non-verbal communication, and resolution is sought before moving on. Verbal communication tends to be indirect.

Low-context communication, on the other hand, tends to be a dominant theme in countries and groups where the wider culture is more diverse. Verbal communication is direct and more meaning is placed on the words spoken than non-verbal cues. Individualism is treasured, and there is much goal-oriented transactional communication in teams.

While these are broad definitions, which can be applied to situations as well as the main groupings I mentioned, the focus for you here is understanding how you can be BRAVE and inclusive when understanding the context of where and who you are communicating with.

It is very possible that you will be communicating with team members who have both of these communication styles. Creating conversations and spaces to understand communication styles, and subsequently getting members of your team to understand how others may perceive and understand the way they communicate, will go a long way in building cohesion in teams.

Interestingly enough, these insights can lead to clarity on my next point – how inclusive leadership can be used to manage conflicts.

Conflict management

No matter how good a team you have, there will be conflict.

Not necessarily the type of conflict that scales from 1 to 1,000 in a moment, but essentially differences of opinion on issues. Sometimes these can be argued about and dissected amicably, and at other times they can cause friction. Your job as a leader is to explore how to handle such conflict within your team or other teams that fall within your realm of influence.

In recent years, I have noticed that a lot of leaders have tried to avoid conflict with their colleagues. They avoid discussion of external politics and they also try to keep the peace by avoiding internal politics. My favourite question when I see leaders who do this is: How is that working out for you?

Here is the thing, I could write a whole other book on how you can manage conflict. But for now I want to give pointers on how best to do this. When faced with a specific conflict – that is, opposing thoughts or ideas – it is good to have a number of tools or strategies to manage it effectively. Whether that be a difference around hiring, how we deal with customers or designing a new product. In the section on 'Mapping product development' in Chapter 5, I spoke about the four 'l's of love, language, listening and leverage when conducting BRAVE conversations.

But even before you get to talking, there are a few things you can do to manage conflict.

You can start by understanding boundaries. Some people can get triggered by the wrong words or non-verbal cues. Set appropriate boundaries in your teams, with consideration of the behaviours that others have shown. This allows team members to show respect for each other and limits the chances of conflict escalating when it doesn't need to.

You can encourage active listening. Rather than people just reacting to others, establish a culture where people can think about how they listen to, and understand, what is said.

Don't avoid tension. When you realize there are issues, you can provide a space for them to be aired out and dealt with, without them festering.

All these things can help build cohesion in your team. You are not going to avoid conflict in teams. Even in very collaborative countries and groupings, there will still be times when you come up against differences of opinion. How you can navigate that sensibly is what I would like to address next.

Antifragility

Antifragility is the ability to adapt, learn and grow stronger through adversity.[20] This is a practice where you and your team work towards a place where you are not easily offended and realize that there will be some tough challenges that

---

[20] N.N. Taleb, *Antifragile: How to Live in a World We Don't Understand* (2012).

you have to face together. The focus is not only on people's strengths but also on their Agility and Resilience to changes.

You want to build an antifragile team capable of embracing change, navigating uncertainty and achieving collective success. Building this requires a deliberate and proactive approach by you and other leaders within your organization.

The world of work has changed so much in the 21st century. In leadership parlance, there is an acronym we refer to – VUCA, which stands for volatility, uncertainty, complexity and ambiguity.[21] It describes the situation of constant, unpredictable change that is now the norm in certain industries and areas of the business world. The challenge for a BRAVE leader is demonstrating how, in such environments, to build teams in which people can not only survive but thrive in the face of adversity.

Teams go through ever-changing circumstances – the introduction of new technologies, economic upheavals, political changes, shifting racial, gender and sexual politics – and very often people are left asking what these things have to do with the job they have been hired to do. The truth is, in this modern era, leaders can't just avoid change and the impact of it on those they are leading; they have to figure out ways to address it.

I am a strong believer that an antifragile team starts with individual members who can view challenges and setbacks as opportunities for growth. Leaders should encourage team members to adopt this mindset by emphasizing learning and improvement, celebrating efforts and reframing failures as valuable learning experiences. They should demonstrate it themselves and then coach others to do the same. By cultivating such a team culture, team members are more likely to embrace change, seek out new opportunities and continuously adapt to the evolving demands of their environment.

---

[21] See W. Bennis and B. Nanus, *Leaders: Strategies for Taking Charge* (1985).

There are some who argue that psychological safety is the foundation of an antifragile team. This means people feel safe to express their ideas, take risks and challenge the status quo without fear of ridicule or reprisal. Leaders are encouraged to foster psychological safety by actively listening, encouraging open communication and valuing diverse perspectives. Team members should be empowered to share their thoughts, ask questions and contribute to decision-making processes. When individuals feel psychologically safe, they are more likely to collaborate, innovate and collectively solve problems, enabling the team to thrive. But more than that, BRAVE leadership also requires people to sit with the discomfort of a differing point of view. This is not carte blanche for people to just say what they want and make claims about freedom of speech. Rather, this is about being Bold enough to encourage Resilience in teams so that they can have difficult conversations.

Inclusive leadership cannot survive in a bubble where everyone agrees. While it aims not to intentionally exclude others, it should also create enough room for dissent and contrasting points of view to shape tough decision-making and make sense of the environments we work in.

Sometimes, clients I work with are terrified of saying the wrong thing. We are never going to get language right all the time. And it is a futile exercise to think that way. However, antifragility is about being BRAVE enough to have those tough conversations and moments of tension, and teams and their leaders being able to work their way through them.

Finally, I believe that leaders who want to foster antifragile teams should get them to actively seek new knowledge and skills, both individually and collectively. Promote a learning culture by providing resources, offering training opportunities and establishing regular feedback loops. As I write, I think of the storm generative AI is causing in the working world. There are a number of legitimate concerns about access to data and the ethics of such technology, but there is also an opportunity for professionals to learn what it is and what advantage it brings to the ways they work. Adopting the polarity thinking I spoke about earlier, what this pursuit of knowledge does is build a range of understanding that strengthens teams.

By nurturing a culture of continuous learning, the team becomes Agile, Resilient and better equipped to handle unexpected challenges.

Of course, none of this is ever easy, and there will often be resistance, so let's explore how to navigate that.

Challenging resistance

While building a system of inclusive leadership for your work environments, you may face resistance from individuals who are uncomfortable with change.

Effectively addressing resistance to inclusive leadership requires understanding the underlying concerns and employing strategies to overcome them.

Communicate the why

Resistance often stems from a lack of understanding or alignment with the team's purpose and goals. Leaders must effectively communicate the 'why' behind decisions, changes and initiatives. Being able to transparently share the rationale, benefits and long-term vision helps to provide context and inspire buy-in. BRAVE leadership is about being able to engage in open dialogue to address concerns and clarify any misconceptions. By connecting team members to the larger purpose, leaders can challenge resistance by reinforcing the shared objective and emphasizing the collective benefits of moving forward. This doesn't mean the resistance will vanish, but it brings a strong business case to move the ideas forward.

Resistance to inclusive leadership also stems from misconceptions, biases or lack of understanding.

I mentioned earlier that leaders should prioritize education and awareness to address these challenges. Creating spaces and programmes that provide insights into the benefits and importance of inclusive leadership is critical. This includes promoting awareness of heuristics and biases, and encouraging individuals to examine their own assumptions and prejudices. And this is not just those mandatory unconscious bias courses, but a well-thought-out process that gets people to understand the mental models and factors that shape how decisions are made through the lens of inclusive leadership.

Through this understanding, clients challenge resistance and show direct reports and other individuals in their sphere of influence the positive impact of inclusive leadership on productivity, innovation and employee satisfaction.

One of the reasons I really placed an emphasis on antifragility is because it allows for creating frameworks where you and other members of your team can address concerns and doubts directly and provide information to debunk myths and misconceptions. It encourages open dialogue and active listening to individuals' perspectives, allowing them to express their concerns and reservations, but without offence. Transparent communication fosters trust, builds bridges and enables a shared understanding of the value of inclusive leadership.

In Chapter 6, I explained how leaders must model inclusive behaviours and lead by example. You should demonstrate inclusive practices in decision-making, team collaboration and interactions with your team. Ensure equal opportunities for participation and encourage diverse voices to be heard and valued. Remember that diverse contributions showcase the benefits of inclusion, but never forget that just because a view may be valid to someone doesn't mean it is vital. This is where you get to model to others that you have taken into consideration a number of differing views but show that the decisions you have made aren't dependent just on one strong view. Rather, you have come to a decision through the lens of many different perspectives.

Accountability

I spoke earlier about establishing clear expectations in your team, and here I would add that you should hold team members accountable for embracing inclusive leadership behaviours. Metrics and feedback mechanisms can help measure progress and identify areas for improvement. Objectives and key results, key performance indicators, feedback systems – all these help to navigate resistance.

You can transparently share data and outcomes to demonstrate the impact of inclusive practices on team performance.

Finally, resistance may arise due to a lack of knowledge, skills or resources required for inclusive leadership. Leaders should provide support and resources to help individuals develop the necessary competencies. Offer training programmes, workshops or coaching sessions that focus on fostering inclusive leadership skills, including empathy, active listening and cross-cultural communication. Create mentorship or sponsorship programmes that connect individuals with diverse role models. By providing the necessary support and resources, leaders empower individuals to overcome resistance and develop the capabilities needed to embrace inclusive leadership.

I try to be as honest as I can and say that this not a straightforward process. BRAVE leadership is damn hard work and takes collective effort. But this is how you shape the culture and move forward if you want to really implement inclusive leadership as a viable model for your teams and ultimately your organization.

Chapter 9

Culture shifts

There is lots of talk around organizational culture and who shapes it. Before I jump into that, let's have some definitions.

Organizational climate and organizational culture are two related but distinct concepts that describe aspects of an organization's work environment. Here's a breakdown of the differences between them.

Organizational climate

This is the overall atmosphere or prevailing psychological and emotional tone within an organization. It focuses on the employees' perceptions and experiences of the work environment, including their feelings, attitudes and reactions. It is *how we feel about policies and practices.*

It is influenced by factors such as leadership styles, management practices, communication patterns and the physical work environment. It is relatively short term in nature and can change based on specific events or circumstances within the organization.

Organizational climate has a direct impact on employees' motivation, job satisfaction and performance. Factors affecting organizational climate include level of trust, openness to innovation, supportiveness, recognition and collaboration within the organization.

Organizational culture

This is the shared values, beliefs, norms and assumptions that guide the behaviour of individuals within an organization. In other words, it's *how we do things around here.*

This represents the deeper and more stable aspects of an organization's identity, shaping how things are done and what is considered important. It is often established over a long period and can be relatively stable over time, depending on the nature of the leadership that informs it. It influences employees' behaviour, decision-making and interactions with one another and with external stakeholders, and it is not easily controlled.

Organizational culture is typically assumed to be shaped by the organization's senior or executive leaders. I would argue that it is the leaders – those who lead through impact rather than title – who are key influencers. It becomes embedded in the organization's practices, rituals, symbols and stories, though these are subject to change depending on context.

~

In summary, organizational climate focuses on the current perceptions and experiences in the work environment, while organizational culture refers to the deeper and more enduring values and beliefs that shape an organization's identity. Both climate and culture play crucial roles in shaping employees' experiences, attitudes and behaviours within an organization.

One of my clients, a senior leader, was frustrated.

She had asked me to come in to coach some of her senior managers because they just weren't getting her directives that she wanted to have a change in the culture. She had spent so much time making sure that staff were aware, through training, posters and monthly missives, what the values and beliefs that formed the organization's culture were. She felt that it was the senior managers' role to not only learn and embed this but also lead by example.

One of the conversations I had with her went like this:

'Have they fed back to you their thoughts on this programme?'

'What do you mean?'

'Let me ask more open questions. Who has fed back to you their thoughts or feelings? When did they tell you? How did they tell you? And yes, these questions are loaded with the assumption that they have spoken to you!'

'Well, I am not the biggest fan of 360-degree feedback?'

'I understand that, but that is not the question I am asking.'

'To be honest, no one has fed back, and I have given them the chance to do so.'

'How can they give feedback to you?'

And so we went back and forth in a conversation where I started to explore the power dynamics between her and the staff. The assumptions around why staff did or did not buy into the culture change initiative. And what she could do to resolve the frustration she had around the lack of response from her direct reports.

Culture change is freaking hard.

Over the years, while working as an employee and as a consultant, and in the work I do now as a coach, I have seen leaders in several industries and sectors try to implement

134 The BRAVE Leader

culture change. It has been fascinating to watch, both from the inside and now externally, how much effort is placed on trying to change cultures, usually by force.

Why is change so hard?

I can honestly tell you from experience and from data from many cultural change programmes that one of the reasons culture change is so hard is that it is very difficult to pin down what culture actually is. Anyone can put up a list of values and claim that this is representative of the culture of an organization, but it is easy to see where this can go south. And then there is the issue of confusing organizational culture with organizational climate. So let's look at what it takes to build organizational climate.

Building BRAVE climates

Building an inclusive organizational climate requires leaders to take intentional and proactive steps to create an environment where all individuals feel respected, valued and included. I am going to reiterate some of the strategies I have already mentioned which leaders can employ to foster inclusivity.

A clear vision

You should establish a clear vision and communicate a strong commitment to that vision throughout the organization, especially taking time to articulate the importance of creating an inclusive climate and making it a part of the organizational values and goals.

Lead by example

Bouncing back to what I said in Chapter 6, you need to demonstrate inclusive behaviour in order for others to follow. And by 'you' I mean everyone across the whole spectrum of leadership. If you are actively engaged in respectful and inclusive practices, such as listening to diverse perspectives, valuing different ideas and treating everyone with fairness and respect, it becomes so much easier for others to follow your example.

Policies and practice

There is much to be said about developing and implementing policies and practices that promote inclusivity. This may include creating non-discriminatory hiring and promotion processes, providing diversity training programmes, establishing mentorship or sponsorship initiatives and implementing flexible work policies to accommodate diverse needs. Beyond talent, this extends to policies around procurement, product design, the customer experience, marketing and board development.

You can measure the effectiveness of these policies by asking the various stakeholders affected by them what impact they are having. Iterate and amend accordingly too.

Open communication

Encourage open and honest communication within the organization. Not the 'open door' policies that too many brag about, but rather flexible opportunities for employees to share their experiences, concerns and ideas. Leaders must actively listen to feedback and take appropriate actions to address issues related to diversity and inclusion.

There are variations in what honest communication looks like across different regions, so shape it with the context in mind, giving consideration to the value attached to hierarchy and the preferred models of communication.

Where possible, leaders can support the formation of employee resource groups or affinity groups, where employees with shared backgrounds or interests can come together, share experiences and support one another. These groups can contribute to a sense of belonging and offer insights on fostering inclusion. And even if there isn't scope for this within the organization, there may be opportunity for this to happen across a discipline or sector. Have a senior leader or leader of influence sponsor and feed back to executive decision makers.

It is wise to regularly assess the organization's progress in creating an inclusive climate. Use pulse surveys, focus groups or other feedback mechanisms to gauge employees' perceptions and experiences. Use the insights gained to identify areas for improvement and take corrective actions.

Remember that building an inclusive organizational climate is an ongoing effort that requires continuous commitment and action. Leaders must prioritize initiatives and polices in all aspects of the organization and lead by example to create a culture where everyone feels valued, respected and empowered.

Influencing BRAVE cultures

One of the things leaders I coach struggle with is my resistance to the premise that organizational culture is merely about setting out values that people are expected to adopt. This is not to say that values have no part to play, but if we are honest, don't people default more to their personal values rather than corporate ones?

A BRAVE culture for me is one where individuals are able to examine all their own varied rituals, behaviours and practices that shape the way they work. For me, these are more important than values that are imposed on you.

When I work with groups, I often do an exercise where I get people to draw a line on a piece of paper. I explain that values are principles or standards of behaviour, a judgement of what is important in life. Having defined what values are, so there is no confusion, on one side of the paper I get them to write a list of their own values, usually the top three. I then get them to do the same for what they know are, or at least believe to be, their organization's top values. Then I get them to match these up to see how far they align.

This exercise of matching personal and corporate values can be a real challenge for many people. Though, anecdotally, I have found that people working in non-profit organizations have better alignment between personal and organizational values than those in other sectors.

As well as there being differences between our own values and our organization's values, it is often the case that your individual principles or standards of behaviour will not be the same as those we lead or work with. And if we all have different standards of behaviour, how then do we all truly align on organizational values just because we are told we must?

However, if we summarize culture in terms of *how we do things round here*, it would largely be shaped by behaviours rather than the notion of shared values. So leaders and their teams shape the culture rather than the other way round.

Before I go off down some rabbit hole on values, let me say they are important but not the key defining pillars of what shapes culture. We only have to look at the corporate values of a number of famous (and infamous) organizations to realize that they don't actually hold that much water.

My advice to leaders around building BRAVE cultures tends to focus on something very different.

Are you really BRAVE?

In the pursuit of clearly defining and articulating the principles that underpin an inclusive or BRAVE culture, ask yourself the following questions:

• What does inclusion look like for us?

- What are our non-negotiables when it comes to inclusive leadership?
- Are we actually BRAVE or do we just play at being Bold, Resilient, Agile, Visionary and Ethical?
- What are the leadership principles that we stand by? (These principles must reflect the organization's commitment to inclusion and serve as a guide for decision-making and behaviour at all levels.)
- Could our staff define what inclusive leadership looks like?
- Does our culture give agency to leaders being BRAVE?

These questions will take some soul-searching. You will probably need to think about your answers over time. But this is a step in the right direction.

Inclusive policies

BRAVE leaders take time to review and revise organizational policies, procedures and practices to see if they align with and promote inclusivity. This includes areas such as recruitment, talent management, performance evaluations and promotion processes. They explore biases, heuristics and models which form barriers that may hinder equal opportunities for all employees.

Leadership DNA

BRAVE leadership has to be universal across the organization. BRAVE leaders foster diverse and inclusive leadership at all levels of the organization and ensure that leaders and managers demonstrate behaviours to support this. They also check for blind spots and actively seek out and develop leaders from under-represented groups so that all the different voices across the organization are heard.

Agency

BRAVE leaders encourage and empower employees to actively participate in decision-making processes. They intentionally provide opportunities for all voices to be heard. They seek to get input from across the organization on important matters and involve everyone in shaping policies and practices that affect them.

In relation to agency in your organization, you could ask yourself:

- Does our workplace culture create psychological safety, where everyone feels comfortable sharing their ideas and perspectives?
- Do we promote collaboration and teamwork across diverse teams?
- Do we encourage employees from different backgrounds and perspectives to work together on projects, initiatives and problem-solving?
- Do we create opportunities for cross-functional collaboration and knowledge sharing?

Learning

BRAVE leaders invest in ongoing education and training programmes to enhance employees' understanding of the power of inclusion. They provide learning and development infrastructure to support the people they lead, whether it be workshops, seminars, coaching or other resources that promote cultural competence and empathy.

Communication

BRAVE leaders foster a culture of open and transparent communication. They encourage active listening and ensure that diverse perspectives are valued and respected. They communicate clearly and consistently about this commitment, with a heart of inclusivity and progress.

Accountability

BRAVE leaders establish accountability mechanisms to ensure progress towards an inclusive culture. They set measurable goals and regularly assess and monitor the organization's diversity, equity and inclusion efforts. They hold leaders and managers accountable for creating and maintaining an inclusive culture.

Building an inclusive culture is a long-term and ongoing effort that requires sustained commitment and involvement from leaders and all other members of the organization. It involves creating an environment where diversity is not only acknowledged but also valued, respected and integrated into every aspect of the organization's operations.

Culture change

One of the more challenging points I see senior executives wrestle with around culture change is that the highest leverage for culture change comes from focusing precisely and deeply on the key influencers – not always those in the most senior positions – whose mindsets systemically affect everyone and everything.

That's right. Culture change doesn't just land squarely on the laps of those in executive positions, but ultimately is driven by those leaders who have key influence and impact within the organization. Touchpoints not titles.

I have worked with clients whose earlier consulting interventions were predicated on the naive assumption that senior people always dictate the culture. They consequently failed to focus deeply enough on shifting the mindsets, attitudes and behaviours of the real key influencers.

When culture change programmes fail from the start, surely this an opportunity for BRAVE leaders to really examine why and ask themselves:

- What are we doing wrong in these programmes?
- Do we actually need a culture change?
- If so, what information are we basing this on?

An organization's culture becomes embedded via the signals people pick up through multiple channels that collectively create and colour their awareness of *the way we do things round here*. I often wonder if people place too much emphasis on culture being homogenous across an organization. But if we are really honest, is the culture in accounts the same as the culture in production? Is the culture in HR the same as the culture in innovation? Is the marketing department culture the same as the tech support culture?

If not, maybe you need to be exploring BRAVE culture through the lens of how all these cultures combine. Rather than trying to make some homogenous culture gloop that says this is how things are done, you should consider how different parts of an organization are symbiotic and work towards a common goal without losing their own identity?

It is easy to bandy about terms like 'toxic culture' and 'culture change' without really thinking about what they actually mean to the people who experience the culture. I would argue that BRAVE leadership is more about examining the habits and practices of various cultures across organizations. Examining how they interact with others. How they align with the vision and mission of the organization and how what leaders do aligns with the leadership expectations across the organization.

I leave this chapter about culture shifts with more questions than answers.

I do believe inclusive leadership can be replicated across any organization. And that once leaders of influence, wherever they appear, understand the principles of inclusive leadership, they will see how this can play a huge role in better decision-making.

Chapter 10

Pulling it all together

The focus of this book has been on being getting you to understand why inclusive leadership works and how it is tied to better decision-making. The aim has been to encourage you to be more BRAVE when facing a series of difficult conversations, handling conflict, solving problems and so on and, ultimately, to influence others to do the same.

In writing this book, I have tried to demonstrate the BRAVE model and the thinking behind my own speaking and coaching practice. I have borrowed ideas and thinking from the practices of other coaches – for example, I mentioned that I am heavily influenced by systemic coaching, polarity thinking and appreciative enquiry. I am also influenced by leading thinkers around behavioural change, cross-cultural communication, power dynamics, anthropology and a host of other areas.

This is a huge work in progress for me. I have seen the impact of this kind of thinking in my coaching practice, but also many others are passionate about the practical application of inclusive leadership.

I am always learning and open to feedback as to how the model works or doesn't work for others. It is one thing to be engaged by individuals and organizations as a leadership coach and come with ideas and observations, but another thing to be respectful of the circumstances, internal and external, that can prevent them and their organizations from being BRAVE.

At the heart of this for me is the desire for people to be more considerate around their decision-making. Wherever leadership appears in an organization, I encourage leaders to be less fearful and more courageous. And I want all of us to learn how, with the right context and circumstances, BRAVE leadership can add value in both a commercial and a personal sense, as well as benefiting the wider communities and environments impacted by our behaviours.

Why inclusive leadership matters

My passion in writing this book has come from my own experience of seeing how exclusionary leadership has left way too many people isolated and marginalized, not only within organizations but also outside of them. So being able to create spaces where people can think about this and act on it somewhat differently than they have done in the past is a challenge I am happy to play a small role in.

This applies whether that inclusive leadership happens in the organizational spaces I tend to occupy most, which are corporate or small to medium-sized high-performing businesses, or whether it happens in the community sector or in health care, environment, criminal justice or education systems.

For me, hearing stories from my clients – and hopefully from others once this book is released into the wild – fires me up. I get to learn more. We get to learn more. We get to lead better.

Making courageous decisions

At the heart of this is my unapologetic desire to see how we as leaders make better decisions, how we can leverage inclusive leadership through the lens of the BRAVE model. I want to interrogate the way we currently explore and make sense of our world, how we approach challenges and, ultimately, how we can make good decisions that we can act on.

There are so many examples of failure to lead inclusively in organizations – commercial, political, community or whatever kind of organization – that are born out of fear. People screw up and are hesitant to be innovative, to think about stakeholders and to do things slightly differently. This is because they work in environments that don't foster or encourage being BRAVE.

This book is a jumping off point for many of us to explore how to be BRAVE.

Understanding leadership through a systemic lens

My second desire is that we as leaders really see leadership through a systemic lens. There will always be greed, misuse of power, corruption and other negative traits that leaders can slip into, but there is also generosity, collaborative use of power, and transparency.

Getting to see leadership as shared, rather than the product of a singular charismatic (or despotic) leader, improves accountability and means that the health, direction and sustainability of an organization is driven by more than just one or two individuals.

It matters that more and more individuals and organizations can see this as a workable means of leading better.

Better management

Past the crude dichotomy of leadership vs management, I realize a lot of people in management end up doing both. How people think that managers are not leaders in some capacity always baffles me, but regardless inclusive leadership lends itself to helping managers make better decisions.

Again, the emphasis here is on the decision-making process. Getting management to leverage tools for decision-making – often tools they hadn't known about – can only be a win for any organization.

But, as I have said, this is not as straightforward as it sounds. People are messy. Even in homogenous groups, when you ask questions to try and find consensus, you realize that people are all very different. What the BRAVE model does is get us to ask better questions around how our thinking and decision-making can be better.

Where do we go next?

I have tried my best to share my thinking around the benefits of inclusive leadership. I have been careful to explore different definitions and to explore leadership through the lens of different cultures and contexts, but I am still very aware that it is not just understanding the principles of being BRAVE that makes a difference – it is putting these principles into practice.

How we get to implement – and measure – inclusive leadership is just as important as understanding the art and science of it.

So what's next?

Sharing stories

We are social animals who love stories. So let's get to sharing them. I invite you to send correspondence directly to me, and I encourage you to share your experiences with your teams and communities or wider audiences.

There are plenty of platforms where you can do that in person, or if you are in a place where opportunities to speak freely are restricted, maybe you can still share stories online. Opportunities to do this have exploded. YouTube, TikTok and Instagram are three popular platforms for telling stories. You can also use podcasting platforms like Spotify, iTunes and SoundCloud.

Personally, I think the intimacy of sharing stories within a close circle of friends or with colleagues – people you lead and those you look to for leadership – is more impactful than hearing something online, but to use polarity thinking, this is a both/and situation rather than an either/or one.

Understanding inclusive leadership in different cultural contexts

I am aware that I have written this book from my perspective as a British man. While I get to work with a variety of organizations around the globe, I am still very aware that, in the main, my work is shaped by British and North American ways of doing business.

So I am curious about the limitations of my model for different cultures. I want to explore more how inclusive leadership works in various countries and cultures. It is all well and good that it works in more familiar contexts, but learning how it works across other cultures intrigues me.

Testing out the coaching models

Having shared some of the coaching models I use, I hope to hear from readers about other models that speak to inclusive leadership. When searching for models relevant to inclusive leadership, I struggled to find resources that go beyond talent management. I also struggled to see examples of this kind of leadership as part of a holistic approach, covering all facets of business.

In addition to exploring different models, I am excited about working with others who will employ the models I have used, who will add their own take on systemic coaching, polarity thinking and appreciative inquiry. I would like to hear from coaches working with clients or organizations who have built their own internal coaching models and practices.

Measuring the impact

Another question I am taking forward is around how we get to measure all of this.

It is great to talk about the benefits of inclusive leadership and have our brains and minds stretched so that we become better thinkers and decision makers, but how do we measure if this thing works?

These kinds of things can be quite subjective, but we can still measure benefits in a methodical way. We can conduct 360-degree assessments, climate surveys, customer surveys and so on. Also, we can try to link this thinking expressly to a return on investment by looking at the benefits achieved against the cost of implementing an inclusive leadership framework.

I have been fortunate to have a few clients who were happy to put measures in place to assess the tangible benefits from coaching on inclusive leadership. But I am aware that leaders in business will want to determine their own ways of measuring this.

Although I left this bit last, I would say it is the most important. Being intentional about how to measure impact is essential if we are to be able to tell the story of why inclusive leadership matters. Whether you want to convince your customers, your staff, your board, your investors or the communities you serve, they will want to know the hows and whys of inclusive leadership.

Finally

It has been very difficult for me to put together all my thoughts on this in this book. If I am honest, by the time this is released, the lizard brain will be thinking about a number of things I probably left out as I tried to get my ideas out there in some comprehensive form. But it is a work in progress and I have had to challenge a lot of my own assumptions from when I first started speaking, coaching and facilitating with clients on the BRAVE model.

As I have become more acutely aware of my own biases and blind spots when approaching leadership development, I realize there are still parts of the model that I need to test more. I will continue to develop my theory of change, and I hope my model will become more robust. If nothing else, I hope there are a few nuggets in the client case studies and the principles I have shared in this book that you can use to be that little bit more BRAVE.

Here's to more of us, as leaders, feeling less fear and having more courage to make better decisions through inclusive leadership.

Sawubona

Recommended reading

These are books that influenced me in writing this book, in no particular order.

Liam Black, *How to Lead with Purpose* (2023)

Nassim Nicholas Taleb, *Antifragile: How to Live in a World We Don't Understand* (2012)

Jeffrey Pfeffer, *Leadership BS: Fixing Workplaces and Careers One Truth at a Time* (2015)

Brian Emmerson and Kelly Lewis, *Navigating Polarities: Using Both/And Thinking to Lead Transformation* (2019)

John Whittington, *Systemic Coaching & Constellations: An Introduction to the Principles Practices and Application* (2012)

Peter Hawkins and Eve Turner, *Systemic Coaching: Delivering Value Beyond the Individual* (2019)

Matthew Syed, *Black Box Thinking: Marginal Gains and the Secrets of High Performance* (2015)

Andrew Sobel and Jerald Panas, *Power Questions: Build Relationships, Win New Business, and Influence Others* (2012)

Peter Hawkins, *Leadership Team Coaching in Practice: Case Studies on Developing High Performing Teams* (2nd edition, 2018)

Barbara Kellerman, *The End of Leadership* (2012)

Michael Bungay Stainer, *The Coaching Habit: Say Less, Ask More and Change the Way You Lead Forever* (2016)

Jerry Colonna, *Reboot: Leadership and the Art of Growing Up* (2019)

Harvard Business Review, *HBR's 10 Must Reads on Making Smart Decisions* (2013)

Acknowledgements

I would love to thank a number of people, in no particular order, who have helped me on this journey.

To Alison Jones and the team at Practical Inspiration Publishing, you kept me going when I literally gave up on doing this. Thanks for your patience and belief.

To my mentor, Liam Black (have you finished yet?), and to Jerry Colonna and Nick Williams, who helped me to put shape to this book and not give up.

To my squad, Paul Boldeau, Adrian McQueen, Remi Ray and Shazia Ginai. Thank you for holding space for me and helping me to keep keeping on.

To Marios, who kept on spurring me on to write and write some more and edit afterwards.

And to the rest of the mandem of MoorHaus – Aaron, Ademola, Alex, Daniel, Darren, Dino, Dwayne, Gary, Jimmy, Justin, Olaitan, Samuel, Sena, Sope, Toib, Toksy, Umar and Viv. You are a brotherhood I am proud to be part of.

To the regular members of The Writing Club who spurred me on with this – Alexandra, Dewbien, Eartha, Iesha, Rosa and Vanessa – and all the other members who have come through for the 7 am writing sessions since 2020.

To the 'Avengers' – Christina, Graham, Jodie, Mark and Sophie. Your encouragement and support has been priceless.

To Mum and Dad for never quelling my rebellious and BRAVE spirit.

Again, Madeline, Rianna and Lauren, thank you for being my everything. I've finally written the book!

Index

About the author

David McQueen is passionate about developing leaders. A family man first, he is husband of one, father of two and friend of many. He has founded and co-founded a number of businesses, including Q Squared, Black Founders Hub and Evermoor, and he sits as a non-executive member on the advisory boards of many companies, offering support on leadership and financial competence.

In his work as an executive coach, facilitator, board advisor and international speaker, he has worked with corporate and non-profit organizations worldwide to develop their senior leaders and managers. His clients include Facebook, Google, Shopify, Lloyds, HSBC, Mercedes-Benz, Sky, BMW, Uber, Fidelity Investments, EY Foundation and Barnardo's.

David is also an angel investor, mentor, host of The David McQueen Podcast and a three-time TEDx speaker, and he never works on a Saturday!

A quick word from Practical Inspiration Publishing...

We hope you found this book both practical and inspiring – that's what we aim for with every book we publish.

We publish titles on topics ranging from leadership, entrepreneurship, HR and marketing to self-development and wellbeing.

Find details of all our books at: www.practicalinspiration.com

 Did you know...

We can offer discounts on bulk sales of all our titles – ideal if you want to use them for training purposes, corporate giveaways or simply because you feel these ideas deserve to be shared with your network.

We can even produce bespoke versions of our books, for example with your organization's logo and/or a tailored foreword.

To discuss further, contact us on info@practicalinspiration.com.

 Got an idea for a business book?

We may be able to help. Find out more about publishing in partnership with us at: bit.ly/PIpublishing.

Follow us on social media...

@PIPTalking

@pip_talking

@practicalinspiration

@piptalking

Practical Inspiration Publishing

Printed in the USA
CPSIA information can be obtained
at www.ICGtesting.com
JSHW072029140824
68134JS00045B/3843

9 781788 604536